CLOCKING OUT

CLOCKING OUT

A Stress-Free Guide to Career Transitions

Raymond Lee

Society for Human Resource Management
Alexandria, Virginia I shrm.org

Society for Human Resource Management, India Office
Mumbai, India I shrmindia.org

Society for Human Resource Management, Middle East and Africa Office
Dubai, UAE I shrm.org/pages/mena.aspx

BETTER WORKPLACES
BETTER WORLD™

This publication is designed to provide accurate and authoritative information regarding the subject matter covered. It is sold with the understanding that neither the publisher nor the author is engaged in rendering legal or other professional service. If legal advice or other expert assistance is required, the services of a competent, licensed professional should be sought. The federal and state laws discussed in this book are subject to frequent revision and interpretation by amendments or judicial revisions that may significantly affect employer or employee rights and obligations. Readers are encouraged to seek legal counsel regarding specific policies and practices in their organizations.

This book is published by the Society for Human Resource Management (SHRM). The interpretations, conclusions, and recommendations in this book are those of the author and do not necessarily represent those of the publisher.

The Society for Human Resource Management is the world's largest HR professional society, representing 285,000 members in more than 165 countries. For nearly seven decades, the society has been the leading provider of resources serving the needs of HR professionals and advancing the practice of human resource management. SHRM has more than 575 affiliated chapters within the United States and subsidiary offices in China, India, and United Arab Emirates. Please visit us at www.shrm.org.

Library of Congress Cataloging-in-Publication Data

Names: Lee, Raymond (Career consultant), author.
Title: Clocking out : a stress-free guide to career transitions / Raymond Lee.
Identifiers: LCCN 2020023379 (print) | LCCN 2020023380 (ebook)
  | ISBN 9781586446543 (paperback) | ISBN 9781586446550 (pdf)
  | ISBN 9781586446567 (epub) | ISBN 9781586446574 (mobi)
Subjects: LCSH: Career changes. | Career development.
Classification: LCC HF5384 .L44 2020 (print) | LCC HF5384 (ebook) | DDC 650.14--dc23

Printed in the United States of America

FIRST EDITION

PB Printing 10 9 8 7 6 5 4 3 2   61.15335

This is for you, Mom.

Contents

Acknowledgments

This book would not be possible without of the support of my entire family. To my spouse, Abby: You have been incredibly supportive of me taking the leap of faith to start Careerminds. In the early days, you maintained the family insurance, a stable income, and most importantly, patience and support. Over the years, my kids Rachel and Matthew have been an inspiration to me for keeping an eye on the ball. I want to thank the late David Freshman and Pat Foley from Innovation Ventures for taking a chance on me and Careerminds. Their investment in an entrepreneur who never took a business class and never started a company before was a risk, and I'll be forever grateful. Jack Gavin, your investment, support, and mentoring of me from the beginning won't ever be forgotten. Justin Schakelman, you are a great friend. You stuck with me in the beginning as I was learning the ropes of entrepreneurship. A special thanks to my former boss and friend JC Gibson for not only supporting my transition to Careerminds, but for being an early adopter and supporter of virtual outplacement. I want to thank all the employees and consultants at Careerminds. I'm incredibly appreciative of your dedication to our clients and participants. Thank you, Kathy Harris, for discovering me at SHRM and introducing me to the SHRM publishing team led by Matt Davis. Matt, you have been a pleasure to work with. Thank you, Josh Hrala, for helping me write this book by bringing the interviews and stories in the book to life. You are a true natural and just get it. I want to thank the late John Connors. John was the first HR professional I came to know in New Orleans who helped guide me through the field of HR and was there when Careerminds was just a thought. I want to thank my brother David for being a role model, best friend, and inspiration. To the late Carol Lagasse, you hired me to my first job in HR and paved the way to my success.

And last but not least, my mom and dad. Dad, thank you for your support of me and for sharing some of the toughest challenges we faced together. Your story and personal experience made this book possible and also helped shape me to be the person I am today, and for that I'll be forever grateful. Mom, thank you for your dedication and hard work as a mother. You're an inspiration to all and your legacy and impact will always live on.

Introduction

Taking on Adversity

Ask yourself: Are you currently in a job or career that is not bringing you fulfillment? Have you recently been faced with a job loss or adversity that is challenging to overcome?

What would you do if you permanently clocked out of your job and your current situation, or if you woke up tomorrow morning and your company asked you to clock out of your job without warning? What would you do next? Every human being throughout his or her personal and professional life will experience some adversity, unexpected change, new opportunity, or simply a fork in the road. The question is "What choice will you make when faced with any of these situations?" Doing nothing is considered a choice, and oftentimes it is made out of fear of what the future holds. After choice, the next question is "What kind of mindset do you possess?" Do you have a growth or fixed mindset? Are you agile? When things aren't working out or are becoming stagnant, are you capable of pivoting and changing direction? Lastly, in the face of the toughest situations and decisions, are you capable of trusting the process and recognizing that you may not know the outcome of your choices? These are difficult questions that we all will encounter at some point in our lives and career.

Throughout the book, I'm going to bring to life four career success principles that can be used when navigating life and career change, whether the change is initiated externally and outside of a person's control or is a decision driven internally. These four principles are:

1. **Choice**—We all have the power of choice. It's accepting responsibility for the actions and choices we make day-to-day and learning and growing from those decisions that is important.

2. **Mindset**—Developing a growth mindset to change, learn, and grow through experience, risk-taking, and application.

3. **Agility**—Learning to recognize when to pivot and change course if something in your life and career is not working out.

4. **Trust**—Recognizing you won't know the outcomes of critical choices when making a decision; you must trust the process.

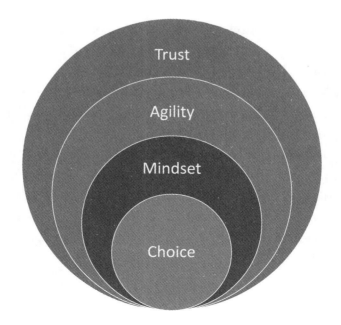

These principles will be highlighted in personal stories that reveal adversity, unexpected job loss, entrepreneurship, and positive career growth and success. At the end of each story, I'll share what I call "Tips for Clocking Out" that are designed not only to help you with career transition but to provide you with encouragement and inspiration. Along with the individual stories, I'll also share my own personal journey from childhood, to college, to the corporate world, and finally to the launch of my company, Careerminds, weaving in each principle that represents that stage of the journey and my career. Every journey begins with adversity and choice; therefore, that's where this story must begin.

It was the summer of 2000, and I was sitting in the living room of my mom and stepdad's home in Gulfport, Mississippi, anxiously waiting for my mom to appear as I prepared to embark on the next journey of my life. My Jeep Cherokee was packed to the gills with my stuff and I was about to leave my home in the Deep South for a new job in Scranton, Pennsylvania, a new, scary destination that I would soon call my home and where I would start my life in HR at Corning. To me, Corning has always been known for its CorningWare dishes, but since the late '90s, they've been more of a technology company, becoming the leading producer of optical fiber in the world. I would be relocating for a recruiting manager position at a new tech start-up plant that made amplifiers to strengthen the signal across fiber optic cables. I really didn't know what any of that meant at the time, but it was an industry that was exploding with growth, and I was really excited about the opportunity.

My mom eventually walked into the living room with tissues in hand. We tightly embraced for several minutes and cried as if we weren't ever going to see each other again. The boy she raised and watched go through challenge after challenge was about to leave his home for a new chapter of life at the age of 28.

Rewinding a bit, I grew up just outside of New Orleans with parents who were both entrepreneurs at heart and went through several career transitions during their lives. My mom was an English major who became a school teacher for many years. My dad spent the majority of his career working in the insurance industry. My parents divorced when I was eight, and my mom, after getting sole custody of me and my younger brother, David, left teaching to work as a court reporter.

At that time, I couldn't appreciate the career move my mom was making from school teacher to court reporter, but later I learned she had a will to provide for me and my younger brother—who was two and a half years younger than me—and was willing to sacrifice a teaching career she loved to pursue something completely different that was entirely unknown to her.

Growing up with divorced parents at a young age had its challenges, and because they weren't around very much I got into trouble quite often. I remember once when I was about ten, I hopped on my bike and rode around the neighborhood, switching everyone's mail to different mailboxes. I'm not quite sure what led me to take on the mischievous endeavor, but it seemed like a fun idea at the time. It ended up not being such a bright idea, as it didn't take long for the neighbors to figure that I did the mail swapping. I didn't switch my own mail, so my mom quickly knew the culprit was me, and they grounded me for a while. I also had to go around the neighborhood and personally apologize to everyone impacted. Apparently, the grounding didn't have much of an impact because later I decided to "roll" the same homes with toilet paper, including ours so that it would be less obvious it was me. It didn't matter because I was caught in the act and found myself in trouble and apologizing for my actions once again. Another time when I was a teenager, I allowed a friend who ran away from home to stay in my backyard shed for several days before my mom found out. I could go on and on for hours with these stories, but I believe the lack of attention led to me getting in trouble. Obviously, this had a major impact on my grades in high school and subsequently led to my teachers and friends thinking I wasn't going to amount to much.

Despite their neglect of me at an early age, my parents' passion for their work taught me the importance of continued education in college. College, in other words, was a must, but unlike many kids growing up today, I didn't get much help from my parents with college planning. I had to figure out where I would go and what I would study on my own.

After some direction from my high school guidance counselor, I decided to attend Southeastern Louisiana University, a small state school in Hammond, Louisiana. I went there for two reasons: it was where I could get in and it was what my parents could afford. I wasn't a great student in high school and was terrible at standardized tests, so getting into a prestigious school was highly unlikely. My initial career plan was to be a counseling or clinical psychologist; hence I pursued a degree in psychology.

Growing up in a city like New Orleans was very interesting. I could literally ride my bike to Bourbon Street and partake in the French Quarter fun as a late teen. New Orleans provided great job opportunities, as the service industry was also my first foray into the job market, working many odd jobs in hotels, restaurants, and the like. Later, when I turned 18, I started working in bars and clubs on and around Bourbon Street while going to Southeastern, which was conveniently an hour outside the Big Easy.

It was a win-win situation! I went to college, came home on weekends, made great money, had a fun time, then went back to school. The bar scene in New Orleans, however, wasn't a positive environment for a young college student. I found myself often spending my weekends with the wrong crowd. Looking back, I'm surprised I made it through my undergrad schooling with above-average grades.

After graduating college, I decided that being a counseling psychologist and working in the medical field was no longer of interest to me. I wanted to be in business and industry. The epiphany came from a visit to a psychiatric hospital where I witnessed patients talking to themselves and verbally fighting with one another. It made me very uncomfortable and I just couldn't see myself happy in that kind of environment. Still, I loved psychology and working with people, but I wanted to be in a corporate setting versus a hospital environment. After doing some research, I learned about industrial-organizational psychology and found it to be the closest discipline that offered a gateway to the corporate world. I applied to several schools and was admitted to Louisiana Tech University where I started my Master's Degree in Industrial-Organizational Psychology. Louisiana Tech is located in Ruston, LA, which is about five hours from New Orleans, far enough for a new start in 1993. I was also fortunate to land a job in the Department of Psychology that helped offset my college tuition, which I was paying 100 percent.

This is one of the first times that I can remember being agile and making a big decision to change my career direction in life. I also had a pretty strong growth mindset at this point, turning my school life around and achieving a 4.0 GPA in graduate school, something that I didn't even know I had in me. I attribute these results to leaving home for a new college environment with new opportunities to learn and grow. I graduated in the winter of 1994 with a 4.0 and was now serious about my future and determined to succeed. My family was all there to celebrate and honor me on my big day.

Then something shocking happened.

On Friday, April 7, 1995, just three months after my graduation, an article written by Bill Voelker appeared in the *Times-Picayune*, the biggest newspaper in New Orleans. It was titled "Jeff Agent Jailed for Mail Fraud." Jeff was short for Jefferson Parish, which is just next to New Orleans and Orleans Parish. The *Picayune* article stated that my dad was being sentenced to eighteen months in federal prison for mail fraud. I couldn't believe it. My dad was going to prison?

It all happened so fast. My dad was single at the time, was an only child, and was not very close to his family, so he didn't have a real support system to help him through this. He didn't have the most stable upbringing as a kid, and he wasn't close to his mother. His biological father was kept away from him for years, so it was just me and my brother, David, who helped him sort things out.

My mom had remarried by this point and wanted nothing to do with his situation. I recall she felt really bad that my brother and I had to be exposed to his shortcomings.

My dad was sentenced to serve an eighteen-month sentence at Eglin Air Force base in Fort Walton Beach, Florida, where he was once stationed in the Air Force. One spring morning, my dad sat me down and requested something from me that still haunts him to this day. There were several requests, actually, all of them nearly impossible for me to say no to.

He first asked if I would drive him to "camp"—a term that he used instead of prison, I guess to make it sound less like a prison sentence and more like a sabbatical. To be honest, I'd probably say the same thing. The second request was that I live in his three-bedroom apartment in Metairie, Louisiana, during the time he would spend at camp to pay his bills and keep his apartment in order until he was released, which would end up being closer to a year as he would get out on good behavior.

The last request was to manage his insurance business, clients, insurance renewals, and claims that would come in on his current policies. Of course, I said yes to all three requests which, just to reiterate, included dropping him off at camp, living in his apartment, and managing his business. Needless to say, my post-grad life was put on hold for the foreseeable future as I worked all of this out.

As planned, my brother David and I drove my dad over five hours on I-10 east from New Orleans to Fort Walton Beach. We arrived at the hotel in Florida the night before he had to turn himself in. That evening and the morning of the drop-off were all tears. My dad was extremely apologetic to us and promised he would make it up to us when he got out. It was one of the most emotional days I've ever experienced. After we dropped him off at the base, my brother and I drove back to his Metairie apartment in complete silence. We didn't say much on that ride home. We were still in shock over everything.

Over the next year, I lived in my dad's home so I could keep his house in order, pay bills, fix things, and keep the place clean. The year I was there was one thing after another. In May 1995, New Orleans and Metairie experienced a major flood and many of the homes in the area were flooded, which wasn't unusual in this area as New Orleans is several feet below sea level. As a result, I had one insurance claim after another coming in. I was on the phone constantly helping clients get connected to adjusters and answering policy questions. By the way, insurance wasn't my thing, so much of this I was learning along the way. My brother and I would visit my dad once a month at camp, so I was able to ask questions and get advice from him along the way.

During this time, I was able to secure a part-time job at a New Orleans hotel working at the front desk and was counting down the days until his release, when I could start my new life. I was 23 years old trying to figure out what I would do when he got out.

Another unfortunate issue my dad faced early in adulthood was relationship issues that had a pretty significant impact on me growing up. He had remarried three times before camp and once after camp, each only lasting a few years. As I became an adult, I found myself experiencing similar relationship and insecurity issues, causing me to have low self-esteem and self-confidence.

I thought to myself, "I'm not going to succeed in life, relationships, or business until I address the issues that keep holding me back." This admission to myself and taking responsibility for myself was a huge step in the right direction, allowing me to be open about what was bothering me about my relationship with my father.

As I thought about my future, I realized that therapy could be a good way for me to address some of my feelings surrounding these facts. So, I was referred to a family therapist whom I saw for two years, which included both individual and group therapy. My therapist, Betsy, was incredibly helpful in getting me to trust and love myself for who I was, helping me to one day recognize that I could be in a relationship and potentially get married—something I couldn't see myself doing at the time.

During this time, I also turned to the Church for community and support. I became a youth minister for a few years at St. Edwards the Confessor in Metairie. The work I did there really filled me with strength, trust, and love, allowing me to truly understand that I had the power to conquer anything the world threw at me if I worked hard enough and trusted that doing the right thing would work to my benefit.

I mention these events in my life not to look for sympathy from others or to shine a negative light on my father, but to simply point out that people are born into situations that are outside of their control. As humans, we are all born into a life where we will encounter some adversity and challenges growing up, some more than others.

Recently, I read Chris Winfield's *Inc.com* article "Want to Change Your Life? Make This One Choice" (April 26, 2016) in which he recounts an interesting story from Dr. Hans Selye, a man who's known by most as the father of stress. Dr. Selye told a true story of two boys who grew up in the same home with an alcoholic and abusive father. Years later, he did a follow-up with these boys, who were now full-grown men, and he found that the two boys were very different later in life.

One of the boys had nothing to do with alcohol. He'd become a professional, respected citizen in his community.

The other one turned out almost exactly like his father . . . abusive, drunk, hopping from job to job, with no real future.

At the end of the interviews, he asked the two men, "How did you wind up the way that you did?" Both answered in the same exact way.

They said, "With a father like mine, how would you've expected me to grow up?"

That's pretty powerful because they were looking at life from completely different perspectives—one from full responsibility and one from no responsibility whatsoever.

Can you see which one of these siblings made the better choice?

In the example above, the brothers' decisions impacted their life, career, and family, and vice versa. How people address adversity is critical to moving forward in a productive manner.

When I think of my own personal life and professional career, I had to tap into all four principles at various stages from growing up, to leading an HR career, to starting a new company. Each major career milestone in my life was a result of the four principles being applied to each stage.

Choice was the first principle I applied early on and the one that led me on a lifelong journey away from home. As I stood in my mom's living room in her home in Gulfport hugging her goodbye and shedding tears with her, I recognized that for me to grow, I had to make the tough choice to leave and begin my career journey. I hope you'll join me for the ride.

Barbara Hester: The Last Dig

"Begin doing what you want to do now.
We are not living in eternity. We have only
this moment, sparkling like a star in our
hand—and melting like a snowflake."

—Francis Bacon

As I set off on my journey to Scranton, Pennsylvania, my mom spent time reflecting on her own life, her sacrifices, and her future. Being forced to grow up at an early age, she also faced some adversity and tough choices, many of which impacted the lives of others. Throughout her life, my beloved mom had my best interest at heart, always putting her kids first and her career second. This didn't occur to me when I was growing up, but as I matured, it became apparent to me that my mom was a true role model and leader to her family and friends. Let's jump right in.

Barbara Thedy Hester was born in New Orleans on February 8, 1952. She grew up with parents, Herman and Joyce Thedy, who never separated and are still alive today. They've been married for close to 70 years and are in their early 90s, still live at home, still drive, and tend to themselves. My mom was a creative person who loved to write and play the piano. Living at home was tough as her parents were very strict on her and her only sister, Carol, who was a couple years younger.

My mom went to high school at Mt. Carmel Academy, a Catholic girls' school in New Orleans, and attended the University of New Orleans where she earned a bachelor's degree in English. She then got married at the young age of 19 to her high school sweetheart, Kirk, after getting pregnant with me. Against her parents' wishes, she married and started a family while attending college. During this time, she also worked odd jobs to put food on the table.

It was tough for her because her husband was in the Air Force and stationed at Eglin, so she didn't really get to see him much. She spent her days writing love letters to the love of her life hundreds of miles away, describing the milestones their little boy achieved. Years later, they had a second son, David, and settled in Metairie, a small town just outside of New Orleans.

My mom's first real job was as an eighth grade English schoolteacher at St. Edward the Confessor, a Catholic school that both of us boys attended. Money was not a primary motivator for her career because teaching was her passion. My dad, after the Air Force, worked in the insurance industry as a sales rep and was the primary breadwinner for the family.

I learned back then that people generally married very young as a way to rebel against their parents and live life on their own. This, too, was the case for my mom and dad, but over time they grew apart and recognized that they were becoming very different people with very different values and interests. This led to them getting divorced eight years later. With my mom getting sole custody of me and my brother, she knew that a school teacher's salary wasn't going to be sufficient for raising two young boys, who were very active in sports and could eat you out of house and home, a saying she often shared when describing our appetite.

When she decided to leave school teaching behind, she took a very pragmatic approach to finding her next career. She needed to find something where she could make a lot of money that also involved English, reading, and writing. She discovered the field of court reporting, or stenography, and learned that it was a very lucrative way to earn an income. After a bunch of research, my mom made the decision that she would attend court reporting school around the summer of 1986 and get her license. Interestingly enough, this type of choice is very common for many people who have transferable skills.

Her **choice** to take a risk to change her career would shape her future in many ways. For one, it would set an example for her kids that you can do and be anything you want if you put your mind to it. She could have remained a school teacher and lived out her passion, received child support and just got by living a simple life. She chose to take a risk and pursue a new career that would provide a better life for her kids at the expense of her happiness. When she received her license and started practicing court reporting, the initial excitement of something new was great. She was meeting new people and enjoying the work.

My mom worked as a court reporter for several years in New Orleans for a few different attorneys, but decided there was more growth opportunity if she left town. A couple of years later, she left and moved herself and her two boys to Gulfport where she joined a small court reporting firm and worked for several years. She never liked the idea of working for someone who benefited from her hard work. The firm would send her on depositions and they kept a pretty high percentage of the fee that was billed to the attorney. She thought to herself, "I could keep all of the fees if I could work for myself." In her mind this was hard-earned money that would put food on the table, send us kids to summer camp, and allow us to take trips together, something we did regularly. She was selfless, always thinking about us before herself. She was truly dedicated to providing for the family and this impacted the choices she made about her career.

She recognized that if she could get enough experience with the new firm in Gulfport and build good relationships with the attorneys she worked for, then one day she could go out on her own and possibly work directly for them. This would afford her the opportunity to really grow and control her own destiny.

During her time as a court reporter on the Mississippi Gulf Coast, she met an attorney called John Hester. John was a well-respected workers' comp attorney who ran his own law practice for many years. He met my mom at the courthouse one day while she was on a deposition. He graduated from Ole Miss and was a diehard Rebel fan. A few years later, on October 20, 1990, they married and lived in Gulfport together.

My mom became one of the most sought-after court reporters on the Mississippi Gulf Coast as she worked hard, traveled quite a bit for depositions, and attended conferences. I remember her telling me once that she went to the annual court reporters conference in the early '90s and met the two court reporters who worked the OJ Simpson trial. I thought that was a pretty cool opportunity. The firms kept her incredibly busy going on several depositions a day. It was a vicious cycle. Her calendar would fill up with work, she'd spend hours and hours working hard to meet unrealistic deadlines, and then the firm would schedule more projects.

She knew it was time to break from the firm to start her business. Making the decision to launch her own business was tough as she was the best court reporter at the firm. They would be devastated to learn of her resignation. This move would prove, however, to be the right decision over time. It allowed her to be selective on the type of projects she'd be willing to take and be more selective of her clients. So, she did just that. She ended up leaving the firm and partnering with another court reporter, launching together Hester and Simpson.

After I left for Scranton, it became apparent that her two boys were completely off the payroll. She realized that court reporting was always a means to an end, and that one day she could consider doing something different. In the meantime, court reporting was still her focus, but changes had to happen. After a few years, she decided to break away from her business partner and work independently and on her own. After reflection, she knew court reporting wasn't her passion and the reality of their company being bigger than the firm she worked for wasn't going to happen. It just wasn't in her blood. As a result, she split from her business partner and began working for herself. I think this separation was the first step to my mom someday retiring from court reporting.

Over time, the work continued to get harder and harder. Court reporting is the kind of job that is tough on the hands and body as you're typing a lot and spending countless hours in front of the computer editing and proofreading. In her early 50s and having spent over 25 years in the court reporting industry, she knew she wouldn't last doing this forever. With her kids now completely off the payroll and on their own, it was time for her to re-evaluate her passion in life and look for a different career.

My mom always had an interest in archaeology. For vacation, she and my stepdad would take trips to Israel with their church to go on archaeological digs with Dr. Charles Page, a scholar on the Mississippi Gulf Coast. She really loved these trips and dreamt about the day where she could leave court reporting and be an archaeologist full time.

With the support of my stepdad, she, at the age of 53, enrolled in the anthropology master's degree program at the University of Southern Mississippi. The school was about an hour north of Gulfport. Her dedication to graduating and working as an archaeologist became her primary motivation. She thrived on an archaeological dig site with her sifting tools, worn clothes, and her disheveled hat to keep from getting sunburnt. The idea of spending her last career doing research and writing about French Colonial archaeological sites was so exciting for her that she was ready and willing to give up a 25-year career that she worked so hard to build from the ground up.

Grad school was a long road for my mom. She made countless trips to USM for sometimes just one evening class a week. She was not able to commit to school full time because her court reporting career was all-consuming.

I remember years after Hurricane Katrina, she was asked by some USM professors to help lead an archaeological dig for a French Colonial site in Biloxi, Mississippi, near the lighthouse. This was a big deal for her as she was able to practice in the field before actually graduating. By this time, she was able to shed some of her court reporting work to focus on the excavation. This was so much more important to her than anything else.

In the fall of 2011, after six years of school, she was getting close to graduating from USM with her master's degree and was actively winding down the court reporting business by only working with a couple attorneys who were really good to her, but eventually had in the back of her mind decided that she'd fully retire by the time she graduated.

At this time in her life, my mom was feeling like she was finally able to enjoy the work she was passionate about. Throughout her life, she always possessed a growth mindset as her desire and passion for learning and growing was at the forefront of her career. She wasn't afraid of taking risks as she recognized that working hard and trusting the process would lead to growth and opportunity. Even when she decided to be a court reporter, she was the kind of person who would make career decisions that worked for her, such as starting her own court reporting business. She may not have loved the work, but she wasn't going to work on someone else's terms; she was going to create a career that worked for her. This kind of entrepreneurship was so impactful to me, who, at the time, was starting college. I saw the choices my mom made and the drive she demonstrated set the direction of her own career path. Little did I know at that time, she chose this 25-year career of court reporting for a better life for us kids, not so much because it was her passion, her calling.

As she approached her final year of her master's degree in the fall of 2011, she completely retired from the court reporting business and finished her last deposition. She defended her thesis, and much of the work she completed on French Colonial architecture was published in several journals and publications. Her departure from court reporting was bittersweet as she left the job and career feeling no loss, no tears, with no regrets. She had put in 25 long years of dedication to a field that was thankless to many and appreciated by few.

She was down to her last semester and spring graduation was near. With all of that hard work in grad school behind her, she shared with her family that she wasn't planning to walk on commencement day. Her commitment to finishing grad school was a goal she had for herself and herself only. The idea of proving to the world that she earned a master's degree was not at all of interest to her. With that being said, at the age of 60, she would be the oldest in her class to graduate. So, with the help of my stepdad, we eventually convinced her to walk across the stage so that her family could celebrate her success.

At this time, I had moved on from Scranton and was living outside Philadelphia with my family and running Careerminds, but I was excited to see my mom receive her diploma. In reality, it was a quick flight and one that I was entirely willing to make. I wasn't going to miss it for the world because my mom was so inspirational and supportive for my entire life.

She was my North Star.

In May 2012, me, my stepdad, my grandparents, and my Aunt Carol all attended her graduation in Hattiesburg, Mississippi. It was a joyous day for all. We were all so very proud of her accomplishment and enjoyed sharing in her success.

Tip for Clocking Out

"Controlling Your Emotion = Making a Better Decision." Despite her emotional tie to her family, my mom made career choices based on personal experience and skill versus a gut feeling. She applied that skill to future careers. For example, after years of writing and being an English teacher, she applied those skills to the field of court reporting, and then to archeology, and was successful.

2

Career-minded: Choice, The Move

"The key to accepting responsibility for your life is to accept the fact that your choices, every one of them, are leading you inexorably to either success or failure, however you define those terms."

—Neal Boortz

Throughout my life, I've learned that choice is all about taking personal responsibility and not blaming others, your family, not having enough money, your upbringing, adversity, or where you may be in life. In order to succeed, you have to take life by the horns, as the saying goes, and own your experience and the choices you make. Do your past experiences shape who you are? Of course they do, but moving forward in a positive way is a choice and it's usually the right one.

I've had some personal adversity early in my life and had to take responsibility for dealing with it at an early age. If I didn't address it head-on, I may have fallen into a similar cycle that would have led me down a different career path than the one I chose, a career path that may have been unfulfilled. The second choice I made beyond the personal healing was to leave the South to pursue a career outside of New Orleans. I personally felt that in order for me to spread my wings and grow, I needed to move quite a ways away from home. For me, this was a necessary choice that was going to be the kind of risk and vulnerability that would build strength and character.

The other important thing to know about choice is that you will never know what the true outcome of your decisions will be when you make them. We will talk a bit later about trusting the process and knowing that effort and hard work lead to success, the mark of a growth mindset. Choice is about taking a risk and stepping outside your comfort zone. There is a saying that "a person grows from what they go through." I learned to always be optimistic and take each career step one at a time and not try to look too far into the future. Living and learning in the present allows you to make great choices for the future.

The choice to leave home and take on a completely new opportunity in Scranton would end up preparing me for the experience I would need to launch my first start-up company, Careerminds. Corning would also be the place where I would meet someone special who would end up being my spouse and silent partner later down the road.

In the summer of 2000 in New Orleans, I resigned from Mechanical Construction Company, where I worked as an HR generalist for four years, and relocated to Scranton to join Corning. There, I accepted a recruiting manager position with Corning at one of their start-up facilities.

Corning, the glass manufacturer, was the leader in low-cost optical fiber technology. At the time, Corning's fiber optics business was exploding and I was tasked with helping hire engineers, managers, production supervisors, and other key salaried positions for a new manufacturing facility, called Benton Park. Some of Corning's key customers were Lucent, Nortel, and Cisco, as they were enabling high-purity transmissions over long haul networks at higher speeds and at a lower cost. For those non-techies, this is a simple way of saying Corning helped make your Internet speed much faster. When I joined the company in August 2000, Corning's stock was over $300 a share and the telecom and dot-com industries were growing at a rapid pace. As a young professional, I'd never experienced a market downturn and I had no idea that the dot-com bubble was about to burst.

Toward the end of 2000, just a few months before the market turned, we were well on our way with filling key vacancies at the facility and getting to full operational capacity. Talented engineers were hard to come by in Scranton, so we used national headhunters to help with recruiting.

In early December of the same year, the plant manager walked into my cube to pass along the resume of a young female electrical engineer from Penn State, named Abby Rossi. Little did I know just how important that person would become.

The plant manager said, "Take a look at this resume when you have a chance. The congressman's office forwarded it to me and asked if we'd consider her for an electrical engineering role with Corning."

I looked up at the plant manager and said "Seriously? She couldn't apply directly with us? She had to go through a congressman for a referral?" I pushed the resume aside and kept working.

After a few weeks, a recruiter we contracted to help generate some candidates sent a bunch of fresh resumes over, one of which was from Abby Rossi, the electrical engineer from the congressman, but this time from a different source. I thought to myself, maybe we should give her a look. After a follow-up from the plant manager, we reached out to Abby and decided to invite her in for an interview.

This talented electrical engineer made quite an impression on the engineering leadership team and recruiters. We made her an offer and she started later that month.

The Engineering department was far from Human Resources, so we both worked at opposite ends of the facility and never saw each other; however, several weeks later, during the holiday party, we sparked up a conversation and started talking. I have to admit, I had no idea when interviewing Abby that I would later be interested in her. Corning was an interesting company in that they allowed spouses and employees who were dating to work at the same facility, as long they didn't report to one another. So at the beginning of the new year, the recruiter and engineer started dating. People sometimes ask me, "Were you really not interested in her when you were interviewing?" I can honestly say, "I didn't know when she was interviewing that she would one day be my girlfriend and my future wife."

We worked together at Corning for just three months before the market crashed.

In early 2001, the plant manager announced a major reduction in force at the facility, saying that the site would probably shut down if things didn't turn around. This meant that now, after hiring and training hundreds of employees for the facility, we were tasked with turning their lives upside down and letting them go. To make matters worse, I, too, was losing my job. This was an incredibly hard time. I had left everything I had in New Orleans to move thousands of miles away for a new career. Now, just six months later, I had no job.

This didn't sit well with me. At all.

It was February of 2001. I remember sitting in my apartment thinking to myself, "What did I do?" The snow was coming down in droves and the thought of spring was nowhere in sight. Growing up in New Orleans, we experienced two seasons: winter and summer, with summer usually coming pretty quickly. In Scranton, winters last an incredibly long time, and with the news of the Corning Benton Park facility closing that year, I was unable to get outside and enjoy the weather to burn some stress and anxiety.

Seasonal depression settled in just like the cold air outside sank into my jacket. It was crippling. When I was let go, I was told my job was being eliminated and that I had a couple of weeks to find another position within Corning or I was getting a severance package.

During these dark days, something great did happen over the first few months of 2001 that helped the situation. Abby and I started dating and fell in love despite the uncertainty of our jobs and future looming ahead of us.

Over the next several weeks, I had to begin networking with other facilities to explore HR roles that I could apply to. One morning, my boss, Julieann Sommers, called me and said there was an HR position at the largest Corning fiber optic plant in Wilmington, North Carolina. I was obviously excited by this new prospect. This could be a huge step in the right direction for me. Maybe, just maybe, my layoff was a blessing in disguise. Abby was also in a similar situation and was looking for engineering positions at other Corning facilities. Abby was offered a maintenance supervisor position with Corning in Blacksburg, Virginia, at a catalytic converter plant. It was a job, but the thought of living in Blacksburg—a city that lay hundreds of miles away—was not appealing to either of us. After talking it out, she declined the Corning offer and accepted severance while I accepted my offer to stay with Corning, so we both moved to Wilmington, North Carolina, in the spring of 2001.

Things continued to be tough for Corning and the telecom industry. In my new role, I worked in an HR department consisting of three consultants responsible for supporting a 2,000 employee facility. The job and the company continued to be incredibly stressful as the future of the company was uncertain.

As Corning continued to have layoffs, the decision was made that Corning HR would manage outplacement internally. Outplacement, as a refresher, is a service offered to displaced workers impacted by a reduction in force that helps them land a new job by providing job search support, interview training, and many other things.

With the number of layoffs that were occurring, it made business sense to leverage the HR organization to deliver these services to employees. Corning branded the internal outplacement program Talent2Talent (T2T).

In Wilmington, North Carolina, a large facility near the plant was set up as the outplacement center for displaced employees to access career transition support. As the HR consultant for the Wilmington facility, I played a strategic role in orchestrating the mass layoffs, coordinating EAP and the newly minted outplacement program.

At the time, having an office to go to was important because not everyone had access to a computer, fax machine, printer, and internet. In-person workshops and face-to-face interview prep rooms were important as we were years away from webinars and video interviewing. Job boards were the gold standard of job search. Monster and CareerBuilder were the big two back then. Desktop computer access with internet capability were requirements for most employees, but many didn't have this access readily available yet.

T2T offices also had workshop rooms for training on interviewing skills and networking sessions. Private rooms were available for phone interviews, resume writing sessions, and coaching sessions. Corning invested an incredible amount of capital to deploy outplacement internally across the United States. They also used Corning employees who worked in HR and recruiting to deliver the coaching, making good use of existing employees.

The one thing that struck me as a challenge here was that because of the amount of employees impacted, it felt like employees were being shuffled through the outplacement center like cattle, receiving little personal attention, which they needed in order to create a personal brand and job search strategy. The other thing I noticed at the center was how some people would come once or twice and never return again. Instead, they would begin to work virtually from home.

I would have never thought back then that Corning's Talent2Talent outplacement center would become the catalyst for Careerminds seven years later. After a few months, Corning started to offer more voluntary severance packages to employees because the business continued to see challenges with the telecom industry.

Despite loving Corning, the people, and the culture, it was time for me to move on. Taking the voluntary severance package without having a job to go to would be scary. I remember thinking, what if I don't find a job or what if my severance runs out? It occurred to me that I needed to trust the process and everything would be just fine. I updated my resume and started on my job search immediately with a focus on moving back to the Northeast. After a short while of job hunting, I was recruited by Ferro Corporation for a plant HR manager role in Bridgeport, NJ. I accepted an offer and moved outside Philadelphia with my spouse, Abby.

Tip for Clocking Out

"Having a Plan B can send Plan A to failure." Since moving to Scranton and leaving home, I've always focused on a primary plan, without really being concerned with a backup or Plan B. This chapter seemed like a series of Plan A's that seemed to fall into place. It became clear that not having a Plan B allowed me to work harder on my Plan A.

3

Kathleen Gowin: A New Sheet of Music

"If I were not a physicist, I would probably be a musician. I often think in music. I live my daydreams in music. I see my life in terms of music."

—Albert Einstein

Careers and life in general both require choices. Despite that, choosing can be an incredibly challenging thing to do. Choice will always be tied up with risk-taking and trust, require agility, and depend on mindset.

All of our choices are different, obviously, depending on the situation. However, we all make choices every day and we all choose where we work, what we go to school for, or even not to go to school at all. Choice becomes a lot harder when the choice you make influences your career and your pathway forward. In order to be able to choose wisely, I always recommend planning and then trusting that plan. Agility will definitely help the process to pivot along the way, but some people are more comfortable with quick choices than others.

In this story, we learn the story of Kathleen Gowin, a risk-taker, who truly exemplifies how to make good, strong choices and have the trust during the whole process to see those choices evolve.

Kathleen was born and raised in Springfield, Illinois, to two working parents. Her father stayed at the same job with a utility company for 35 years before retiring. She is the second oldest with an older brother and a younger sister and brother.

In her early life, she was a member of a small singing group following the format of the national group, Up With People. Small communities would take high school students and teach them singing and choreography with a small band. They sang uplifting (but not religious) tunes about how people can work together and make a better world. Eventually, after being with the group for a few years, the pianist in the group left for college, causing there to be a need for a replacement.

Kathleen wanted this vacant role really badly but had one problem: she had no clue how to read music. Still, that wasn't going to stop her. She would take a tape recorder, record every bit of piano playing she could, and then study it at home. Using this method, Kathleen was able to learn around 20 songs with no formal training, which got her thinking, "If I can do this with no formal background, what else could I do?"

With this thought in mind, Kathleen entered college at Northern Arizona University to study music, specifically piano. She was 17 and leaving home on a new journey, a blank sheet of music ready to be written.

Kathleen says that this is the first time in her life where she realized that she embraced change. She believes that at that tender age she got a glimpse of herself as a person who not only deals with change as it comes but actively seeks it out, a part of her personality that has been true throughout her career.

Kathleen was the first person in her family to graduate college, although she says her dad quickly followed suit. At the age of 40, he managed to obtain a degree in public administration from the very same university where she attended graduate school.

While at school, Kathleen double majored in music and political science, though she dropped music down to a minor to finish school on time. Around this time, she also started taking business courses because she wanted to ensure herself a job, which can be quite hard to pull off with a poli sci degree.

After undergrad, she was accepted to the prestigious Thunderbird International School of Business. However, tuition was expensive, and the school also required a language proficiency that she lacked. So instead, she decided to turn down the offer and enroll at the University of Illinois, where she obtained her MBA.

With her degree in hand, Kathleen landed a great role with the State of Illinois. While there, she helped create and develop the Deferred Compensation Program, which involved her determining operational procedures, the enrollment process, and many other things. Again, Kathleen was excited to have a new blank music sheet right in front of her waiting to be figured out. She goes back to this metaphor often, stemming from her music days.

She worked this role for eight years, working with over 5,000 participants during her time there. For those who need a refresher, deferred compensation plans help workers save money in various ways. In its simplest form, the plan withholds part of an employee's paycheck on a pre-tax basis for a future date—retirement, for example. There's a lot to be said about these types of programs, but we'll leave it at that for now!

Kathleen's manager was in charge of creating this program and turned to Kathleen to create the operational processes. Together, they managed to increase enrollment and help workers understand the program in general. This means that Kathleen got an absolute ton of public speaking time, helping her iron out a new skill while also getting to meet people all over the state.

All of this was happening while Kathleen was around the age of 21. Back then, she felt more like an entrepreneur trying to get people to use this new program rather than a state worker.

After eight years of developing the program, Kathleen started to feel like she wasn't progressing anymore. The department, now staffed with ten employees, was running smoothly and quickly bringing in more participants. It was time for a change. Time to learn something new.

As luck would have it, Kathleen's father knew someone who was the chief financial officer (CFO) of an Illinois-based bank. The CFO introduced Kathleen to a senior vice president (SVP) that had a job in mind for Kathleen: sales.

Kathleen had never wanted to be a salesperson. In her mind, salespeople were the guys in plaid shirts trying to sell you a lemon at the car dealership. She turned the offer down. A few weeks later, the same SVP called and said that they had a job that was "about identifying a customer need and then seeing if the bank's got a product or service that can fill that need or close that issue."

Excited, Kathleen jumped on the role. However, as you probably suspect, it wasn't a different role at all. It was the same sales role that she passed on before.

After some back and forth with the bank, Kathleen accepted the job. Once there, she was asked to do pretty much the same thing she did for the State. There was a new product offered by the bank. Kathleen had to develop this product, find a target market, and make some sales. She was, in short, doing everything, and was allowed to figure it all out on her own.

In Kathleen's mind, the position at the bank was very similar to her old role. It didn't even really feel like a career transition. Instead, it was more like a different side of the same coin. This, obviously, enabled her to flourish in the role, though it didn't provide as much opportunity for her to grow going forward.

Thinking about her next move, she decided that she wanted to continue in the investment space. To get a new role, she took a rather different approach than most: she presented at a conference on a new product that the bank had produced under her guidance.

This conference, unbeknownst to her, had some very high-level people in the audience. One of them happened to be from the huge consulting firm Deloitte. Right after her talk, the person came over to her over her, saying how much she valued what Kathleen was talking about. In fact, as luck would have it, Deloitte was attempting to do the very same thing at their organization and needed a manager to pull it off. Kathleen was the obvious choice after her work with the State of Illinois and the bank.

There was one hurdle, though. In order to work for this Big Six firm, she would have to split her time between Springfield—after moving around the country for a bit during her grad school years— and Pittsburgh, Pennsylvania, where the firm wanted her to be.

The idea of moving to Pittsburgh wasn't appealing to Kathleen. The city was still gritty, dirty, and polluted, though it had cleaned up its act a lot since the steel mill days. Still, it wasn't a good fit. This meant that Kathleen had to travel every week to be at the client's location while still living in Springfield.

The grind, which was bearable at first, soon started to wear on her. Still, she performed her duties for three years. Then, an IRS decision came down from the government.

Kathleen says that the IRS made a decision that consultants who travel every week to their client locations were the same as people commuting by car to an office in the same town. This meant that companies and employees were not allowed to deduct travel expenses to the client site from their home city, even if they were traveling by plane.

Obviously, this directly impacted Kathleen's employment. The new rules were confusing and cumbersome. She had a few options: move to Pittsburgh, move to the actual client site (which moved every year), or leave the organization.

After weighing her options, she decided to leave Deloitte and look for a new role. The year, at this point, was 1996, the start of the dot-com era. Eventually, Kathleen managed to land a job at a bank in Charlotte, North Carolina.

Here is a prime example of Kathleen being agile. She saw her opportunities at Deloitte and made a quick decision. A good one, at that. Charlotte was on the cusp of becoming a banking mecca, and the bank she landed a role with was the first to have a nationwide, coast-to-coast presence. It was a perfect fit.

During this time, the bank she was working at was basically trying to become the McDonald's of banking. They wanted to stretch across the country and provide the exact same experience for every customer. To pull this off, the finance group needed Kathleen's project management skills to work with acquired banks and move them on to the bank's finance platform. After several such bank acquisitions, she developed a software platform to manage the 65 team members deployed on multiple projects, enabling more efficient use of time and resources.

This was a huge undertaking, but Kathleen managed to pull it off. In fact, she was so good at it that she even pitched the idea of launching her own company to a coworker. They could figure out all of the technical stuff, write a methodology, and sell it. Her coworker wasn't ready to take such a risk, so Kathleen kept taking on traditional roles instead of branching out into her own business.

After performing this role for around three years, it now being 1998, Kathleen pivoted again. This time she took on a new role internally at the same bank in order to understand how banking worked on an internal level based on economic factors. Basically, she was leveling up her knowledge. At the same time, she was managing products that correlated directly with changes in interest rates announced by the Fed.

As rates moved up and down, she had to come up with solutions. This meant that she had to basically learn how to predict what the Fed was going to do. Were they going to up rates? Lower them? What were the leading indicators? She also had to figure out how to handle the fallout from 9/11 when planes were grounded for four days. How were her clients supposed to get through this when banks relied heavily on planes to clear checks around the country?

Needless to say, Kathleen's experience at the bank was enlightening, engaging, and full of a growth mindset. She performed tasks, managed clients, and developed products, growing with every turn.

Her next role was at a very large Wall Street bank. She was headhunted for this role, though. It would have her moving to Florida. She was worried about all of these moves. She had started with Illinois and hopped around over the course of a few dozen years. That can often oftentimes look poor on a resume. Still, this chance was a no-brainer. It was a huge bank, and if nothing else, her resume highlighted her upward progression through the banking world.

This new opportunity also provided yet another way for Kathleen to stretch her wings. During this time, many payment transactions were still handled by paper checks. After 9/11, it became clear to banks that something had to change because the technology was now at a place where electronic banking was possible.

The change to the Florida bank provided a way for Kathleen to learn everything about electronic transfers and how they worked because she was on the ground floor when it came to implementing them. Her role, summed up in as few words as possible, was to help migrate clients onto the bank's electronic systems. This is all very complex and beyond the scope of this story, but if you're interested in learning about banking during 9/11 and even the hurricane seasons that followed, it's well worth your time!

Anyway, Kathleen worked this role in overseeing migrations with other banks, but after these were completed, the job became dull again. She wasn't progressing the way she wanted to anymore and felt like it was a good time in her life for a change.

In another agile move, she contacted a friend of hers who was now in corporate recruiting for the bank she left in Charlotte. As it turned out, they were looking for someone for a treasury management role that was open. Kathleen loved her time at this bank and quickly made the decision to move back to Charlotte to help out.

Her husband, whom she married back in 1996 and who also had a career in the banking industry, packed up and left Florida, glad to have the hurricanes behind them.

Once in Charlotte and settled into her treasury role, she was asked if she'd be willing to oversee relationships with title companies and mortgage lenders. This was 2006–2007. Kathleen, with all of her housing market knowledge compounded by the fact that a condo she had just sold in Florida lost about 40 percent of its value, smelled something in the air. There was going to be a huge bubble burst soon.

She could feel it!

She turned down the role after expressing her concerns over the market. You know what happens next. The housing market implodes and the United States is sent straight into a recession.

However, sensing a great opportunity, Kathleen took the role and found herself developing processes and controls to protect the bank from losses resulting from client bankruptcies. As behemoth bank after behemoth bank failed, she managed to keep her division from taking losses, earning her much respect from the entire company.

In fact, she was so good at her role that she was tapped by the bank to manage the relationships in other countries, many of whom were about to have the very same struggles as those in the United States, to keep them from failing as well. This was a huge task. One to definitely get the blood moving. Kathleen was thrust into the global banking world.

"I think what many people don't realize is how close we came to an economic collapse of the financial system worldwide," she said. "It really was a very unusual time, and there were no clear answers, and there were a lot of people who would step back and just try to protect their own interests and not think about the bigger picture."

Kathleen worked this intense role for about 18 months and saw her peers in other banks impacted by the change. This was because regulators in countries around the world wanted local executives, not a global executive who lived in the United States. Her bank began dividing the global territory into five major regions, and she did not want to take on diminished responsibilities.

This was an incredibly stressful time for Kathleen. She was pushed to her limits. When she did eventually leave, it was to become the interim president and CEO of the Bankers Association for Finance and Trade (BAFT) in Washington, DC, a very lofty position. However, she took this role knowing she would move on.

In fact, she even told them when she took the role that she wanted one day off per week to look for a different job. They agreed. The main reason she wanted it this way was because she knew it was an interim role where someone else would step in sooner or later to fill it permanently. She didn't want to give up control of her destiny, so she made a deal. This is, again, a hallmark example of choice and agility. Kathleen looked at the role, looked at her future, and made choices very quickly. She only worked at BAFT for six months before landing another role at a global tech company.

Kathleen was asked to take this firm's existing technology and apply it to banking. After all, she was perfect for the job with her past experience. The happy days didn't last long.

In 2014, after only being at the company for two years, a new CEO was brought on who didn't share the same vision. He didn't want to spend a bunch of money to get the company involved with banking. The solution? Dissolve the entire department, which included Kathleen's job.

Given her agile spirit, she was ready for the change. Kathleen started working with an outplacement firm and career coach on what she was starting to believe was her true passion: her own business.

For much of her career, going all the way back to her first stint at the bank in Charlotte, she had figured that she had what it takes to launch a successful business. And as she absorbed more and more knowledge through these other positions, she finally felt like she was truly ready.

Kathleen pushed ahead with determination to start her business, another sheet of music. This is likely because of her mindset, which is always looking forward, growing, and learning. In fact, she told me that she was already considering what her next step would be even before the CEO shut down the division.

"I knew that's what I wanted because it had clearly been something I had been thinking about. But it also meant my husband and I had to be sure we were on a strong financial footing," she said.

So, with a new goal in mind and a career coach to help her through the beginning growing pains, Kathleen started her own business that sold to banking consulting firms. This is where Kathleen learned all about trust.

Trust, for an entrepreneur, is vital. If you have a coach, you have to trust a process. If you do not have one, you make a process and trust yourself. Either way, trust is key because you can't keep second-guessing every single decision or no work will get done. This is the same for any job transition. There's always a process to be followed and trusted as long as you take care to develop one, or work with someone who can lend you a hand.

For Kathleen, the process was clear at first: set up an LLC, create a website, and generally make all of the typical business entities needed to jump in. However, the biggest challenge was switching from being a recruit to being a business. In other words, Kathleen had to learn to sell herself, which was the same as selling the business.

This meant that she had to stop acting like someone looking for work when pitching to other companies and instead pitch her services as a product, like she did when she already worked for a bank. A mindset shift like this isn't easy to pull off, but thanks to her coach she had a good support system helping her out.

Three years in, she experienced one of her biggest hardships. Deals just weren't coming in like they used to. What was going on? Was it her? Was it the company she built? These questions can drive a person mad, but Kathleen dug in and did some research. She found that the economy was just softening right now for her services. She had to ride this out.

So, again, she trusted herself. She trusted that this was just a hardship and that she'd come out the other side. This is another vital thing for a business owner to understand. Not every quarter is going to see exponential growth, but the long term usually does if you are doing something worth selling (you'll figure out quickly which side of that spectrum you're on in the early days).

Those days are now behind her. Kathleen is now five years into her business and continues to work for herself, a position that—despite what some of her friends and family say—is not retirement. She still works and has no plan on stopping anytime soon. In fact, she's the only one of her siblings that isn't currently retired.

Kathleen, throughout her career, created masterful pieces of music and made agile, forward-thinking decisions that took her from studying political science and music into the upper echelon of the banking world. At every turn, she looked at what was still ahead, asking herself how she would grow, is it time to move on, what's next, and then what's after that? Her process, one that she definitely trusted from start to finish, was based on agility, choice, and mindset.

Without all of these key attributes, she very well could have stuck it out in lower positions and made a happy living, but she didn't. She had a thirst for more.

Tip for Clocking Out

"Entrepreneurs are born, not created." Kathleen spent her entire career solving financial problems for the companies she served. She knew one day, this experience would lead her to launching her own consulting business, a mindset that never faltered.

Karen Stevens:
The Road Less Taken

*"Do not go where the path may lead, go instead
where there is no path and leave a trail."*

—Ralph Waldo Emerson

I met Karen Stevens at a HR conference several years after starting Careerminds. During her career, Karen worked for another start-up outplacement company that competed directly with Careerminds. She was their number three employee. As I got to know Karen and her story over the years, I was amazed at all that she accomplished, the pivots she made in her life, and where she is today.

Karen's story features tons of quick choices: the choice to follow her passions, to always move forward, and to take risks. Through her choices, Karen's story also features many different principles described in this book, but they all come back to that central point: choice.

Karen Stevens was born in central New York just outside of Syracuse. She was the oldest of four. Karen says that she had as close to a storybook childhood as possible. Sure, there were issues, everyone has them, but she fondly remembers playing outside until nightfall with other kids. Her house's backyard was against a cornfield, giving the whole scene a bucolic nature.

Around age 12, sometime in middle school, her family packed up and moved to Alabama. She's quick to note that her experience moving wasn't how it sounds. Typically, people think "New York" and immediately conjure up big city. This was not the case. Her family lived a pretty rural life. When they moved to Alabama, a place that most people associate with farms and rural living, they moved to a bigger city. So, it was the reverse of how most people think.

Though Karen's family still clung to their New York state roots, visiting the family cottage in the summer months, moving to Alabama was a culture shock. The family had to move there because Karen's father, who worked as a computer salesman back in the days when computers took up whole rooms or more, had a new opportunity there.

After three years, the family moved again, this time to Houston after her father got a promotion. All this moving around seems like it would have been a burden on Karen, but she was looking forward to the move to Houston to get a fresh start in a new place.

Once in Texas, Karen joined up with the drill dance team and loved performing during halftime at football games. She says that she was close with her family, though her sister and her were a little more distant until later in life when they both got married and had children at similar times. Still, family life was generally good throughout high school.

Then Karen decided to take a risk.

At the age of 20, she packed up her little white Chevette and drove, by herself, to California. She was a junior in college at this point and she was looking for a change. As an aspiring actress, she had always dreamed of living in California, and so, chasing her dreams and a certain love interest, she set out for the west coast.

To make her move, Karen applied to small liberal arts colleges, specifically ones with good theater departments. Back in high school, her school's theater troupe was top-notch, getting reviewed by local papers and everything.

This may make you think that Karen was an ultra-outgoing person, but she says that she was shy. Very, very shy. Theater was a way for her to break out of her comfort zone. Even this early in the story, this is a clear example of having a growth mindset. Doing things that make you feel uncomfortable for the sake of beating them and improving those skills is a very challenging thing for anyone to do. Still, Karen was very successful at it. In fact, when she landed her first role back in high school, she was as comfortable as ever on stage in front of hundreds of people. It was like a switch was turned on at that point.

After hunting down the right school, she attended a small Catholic liberal arts school and majored in theater. Once she graduated in 1991, she worked as a receptionist at a start-up biotech company and did theater at night. Though she loved it, she never saw herself making enough money at theater full time, as it would require a lot of sacrifices, so instead, she worked jobs and continued her passion outside of work.

One day in 1996, she realized that she had outgrown the theater. She laughs as she says that it's kind of ironic that that is when directors were starting to take notice of her. But, she says, they all wanted to make movies and things like that. She had never wanted to become a film actor so she had no trouble turning them down.

Still, back in the early '90s, Karen's story is full of agility. She was working at a biotech company during the day, doing theater at night, and still looking for direction. She decided after much debate to go back to school and get a master's in psychology because, at this point in her life, she thought she wanted to be a therapist.

This type of thinking is ultra-common among college grads. Sure, you go to school for something particular, but that doesn't always translate into a career. For Karen, she now held two degrees, and she didn't really want to use either of them. She dropped the notion of becoming a therapist, for example, after having to do a practicum at school, which involved doing actual therapy work. What she found was that she loved the theory and bookwork of it all but hated the practical application.

To make matters worse, to become a full-time therapist would take about three to four years of unpaid internship work to amass enough hours to get certified. That's three to four years with no income from a job that is full-time. To make ends meet, Karen would wait tables, a job that didn't pay well at all but that she liked regardless. She soon pivoted her ambitions of becoming a therapist and waited tables full-time for a while.

This is a prime example of trust. Karen just spent about $30,000 on a degree that she didn't want to use. She wasn't sure of the next path to take, but one thing she knew was that she was going to do what made her happy, knowing that she'd figure it out. This is the same mentality that she had when she transferred what she was doing and moved from Texas to California with only her car.

Then, one day while waiting tables, two regulars came in and requested to sit in her section. She made some friendly talk with them like she always did, and the conversation eventually turned to her stepping down from her therapist training because she didn't like it all.

The woman she was talking to then told her that she'd be perfect for sales. Karen was shocked. She asked, "Why do you think I would be good for sales?" The woman replied, "Who in the restaurant gets the greatest number of requests from regulars to sit in their section?" Karen replied, "I do." The woman said, "That is sales. We're repeat customers to you."

Even with their observation, Karen was still not sold. There was no way she was about to become a salesperson. She didn't want her father's career and, back then, sales meant getting in your car, dropping off business cards, and things like that. None of it was appealing to her.

The woman asked Karen to stop by her office to check out a few opportunities she was trying to fill. Out of courtesy, she went into the woman's office and heard her pitch. She wanted Karen to work either selling pharmaceuticals, which was more like being a marketing person than it was being a true salesperson, or copiers, which was definitely a typical sales role. Karen hated both ideas. In fact, the thought of performing any of these roles made her sick to her stomach.

Again, out of courtesy, she went back into the office and told the woman that she just can't take these roles; they're not for her. To her shock, the woman said, "Good!" After a baffling moment, she said that instead of Karen working as a salesperson for another company, she should work here with her.

Karen accepted! She was around 28 or 29 at this point, entering the workforce in an entry-level agency recruiting role. She worked there for about 18 months getting the hang of things and then left to become a contract recruiter for a tech company right around 2000, an era better known as the dot-com bubble.

She managed to keep her role as a recruiter throughout this time period but was still laid off in 2002, an event that was made worse by the fact that her husband, whom she married back in 2000, got laid off at the same time. In fact, both of their roles were eliminated within two weeks of each other.

To patch over this desperate time, Karen turned to an old love: weight loss. A few years before, Karen and her friend joined up to lose a few pounds and were smitten with the idea of helping other people lose some weight the same way, even though her goal was nothing extreme, just 10 pounds or so. Still, the idea was there.

Over those few years, she worked part-time for a weight loss company, which only amounted to a small amount of money and, in her words, didn't even really feel like a part-time job at all—more like a volunteer role.

When her second child was a few months old, a funny thing happened: the VP of HR from the company that let her go three years before gave her a call. They were looking for someone to oversee their recruitment at the company on a part-time basis and her name came up. The role would be about 20 hours per week with good pay and mostly involve working from home, so it would allow her to have the work/life balance she needed. She took it immediately.

She worked there for a few years before another hiring freeze forced her hand. She then tried working for some recruiting agencies, but agency life just wasn't for her. After a few years of pursuing different paths in talent acquisition, an interesting and compelling path opened up before her. A role with a tiny start-up company focused on getting people back to work during a recession. Using her skills as a recruiter, she managed to land the new role. She was so excited! While there, she got to use her unique ability to create a role for herself. She managed the hiring of other recruiters—who she knew were all out of work in 2008 and 2009.

Karen's experience up to this point was the culmination of many interesting choices and pivots. It started with a move to California to pursue a theater career, then after five years, it was psychology and becoming a therapist. Later, it was sales and recruitment. Karen was a risk-taker and true entrepreneur. She was able to bring together all of the pieces she learned from her career to make this start-up successful. The company allowed her to truly flourish. She was able to switch into an executive leadership role, which took advantage of every aspect of her background. In short, she was thriving there. It seemed like all of her skills were coming together in unique ways. She loved her job!

Despite the success of her role, what truly kept her there was an excitement and entrepreneurial spirit that pervaded the company. But that spirit often wears off. In 2015, it did for her. She was no longer able to fix problems, start new products, or innovate in new ways. Instead, it became business as usual with the company focusing on their "bread and butter" and not the next big thing.

The straw that broke the camel's back was when the board pulled the plug on a major project she was leading, which really took the wind out of her and led Karen to make the choice to leave the company.

At the same time, Karen's father died suddenly, prompting her and her husband to rethink their priorities and what they wanted. They considered moving to Texas to be closer to his family. She shared with me that her husband's parents were getting up in age and they would totally regret something happening to them and not having the opportunity to spend time with them. She said, "Life is short, and the sudden death of my father put a fine point on that saying." Karen and her husband made the decision that they would move back to Texas and leave California.

In 2015, when she began her search for jobs back in Austin, Karen started looking for roles and networking while still working for the company. It turned out that someone on her company's advisory board was able to help her out by spending time with her to work on the job hunt. This person was well respected in the HR community and was willing to help spread her resume to his trusted network. Karen was not only appreciative of his help, but was moved and touched that he *wanted* to help. She clearly recalls feeling very grateful that this person in a high-powered environment took her under his wing and made connections that he really didn't have to make. It turned out that every person he emailed got back to her.

Karen was primarily focused on Austin, Texas. Two of these jobs from the introductions made the cut. One of them was to be a cofounder for a tech start-up. This would require her to figure out the product, pitch to investors, and really allow her to grow. The other opportunity was very different and was with a global consulting firm. She was torn on which path to go, another huge choice to make and probably the most important at this stage in her career. As she was thinking about her decision, she had a call with one of the contacts that her advisory connection made to her. They talked for a few minutes and Karen described the two opportunities to her. The networking contact said, "I've only known you for a few minutes and can really appreciate your struggle on which opportunity to go with, but can I offer you my two cents?"

Karen replied, "Absolutely."

She said, "Knowing your background, it makes perfect sense for you to go with the small company because of your start-up experience. It's your comfort zone, but the other opportunity which is with a global company is the kind of opportunity you've never experienced. I feel that the global company would be the right decision."

Karen replied, "That is really great advice!"

After thinking it over, Karen accepted the global role. It has been five years now, and I asked Karen if she knows where the start-up company is today. She thinks they no longer exist. She often thinks about whether the start-up would still be around if she decided to go there instead. She made her choice and has never looked back since. She is still in the position today and is very happy.

Tip for Clocking Out

"Life is too short to be anything but happy." Karen lives life to the fullest. She's made many life changes, big moves, and bold starts and has never looked back. She's also never been afraid to rely on her trusted friends and network to provide support and guidance along the way.

Career-minded:
Mindset, HR to Entrepreneur

*"All our dreams can come true, if we
have the courage to pursue them."*

—Walt Disney

As far back as I can remember, I've always had a desire to be an entrepreneur. I think it started back when my mom left being a schoolteacher and became a court reporter and then started her own business. I recall seeing her get her own business cards with her stationery, typewriter, and court reporting machine, which, if you didn't know, is a strange-looking keyboard that appears nearly impossible to use to the untrained eye.

At the same time, I've always had a passion for helping people figure out their career direction and offering advice. When I had my first job in New Orleans, I used to attend the Society for Human Resource Management's (SHRM) student chapter meetings and present to the students on career planning, resume writing, and interview preparation. I enjoyed helping them think about their careers and what was possible.

While my time at Corning was a real driving force in terms of what Careerminds would be and do, back in 1996—while I still worked at Mechanical Construction Company in New Orleans—the real "work" of creating Careerminds began. Back then, the internet was booming, literally. Everyone was buying up dot-coms, trying to get specific names before someone snatched them out from under them.

So, one day at work, while I was sitting at my desk daydreaming about running my own company, I decided I should go ahead and purchase a domain name. That long ago, there wasn't a GoDaddy you could go to for a $10 registration. I had to call an 800 number, sit on hold for a few minutes, and finally speak to a real-life person.

I recall thinking about what my domain name was going to be while being on hold. Because of my desire to help people with job searches and resumes, I wanted something with "career" in the name. I asked the agent on the phone if career.com was available, and of course, it was taken. So then I started putting words together with "career." Eventually, the "minds" part of the name came from me having a psychology degree.

At that moment, it hit me: having a career is a state of mind! It is more than just having a job. It's a mindset that a person possesses that is a lifelong journey of thoughtful growth, continued learning, risk-taking, trust, and hard work.

The concepts of mindset cannot be discussed without mentioning Carol Dweck and her book, *Mindset: The New Psychology of Success* (Ballantine Books, 2007). In her book, she describes the difference between a growth mindset and a fixed mindset, showing how success in your career can be influenced by how you think about your talents and abilities.

Taking a risk, embracing change, and accepting the Corning severance package represented a growth mindset. The fixed mindset would have led me to stay and not try something new. I would have continued to work at Corning and accepted that the economic misfortunes were dealt to me and I should just accept it. Over time, I may have gotten laid off and would have been forced to make a change. Basically, a fixed mindset equates to career stagnation, because you've stopped learning and giving effort to self-development.

The growth mindset, on the other hand, assumes that everyone can change, learn, and grow through experiences, risk-taking, and application. The challenge with risk-taking and experience comes from the threat of failure. Growth mindset thinking sees failure as not a detriment, but an opportunity for success.

In her book, Dweck writes, "After 30 years, my research has shown that the view you adopt for yourself profoundly affects the way you lead your life. It can determine whether you become the person you want to be and whether you accomplish the things you value."

What is ironic is that the name Careerminds came to me primarily because of the blend of my psychology degree, which is the study of the mind, and my passion for careers. It wasn't until later that I started to learn about the difference between having a growth mindset and a fixed mindset when applying to careers. So Careerminds was the name, and the tagline for the company later became "Thinking about your future."

By now, I had been working for Ferro for several years as the plant HR and living in South Jersey, just outside Philadelphia. We had our first daughter, Rachel, and Abby landed a new electrical engineering position at W. L. Gore and Associates based in Newark, Delaware. I continued gaining beneficial human resource experience at Ferro, but was getting antsy to do something else. I had accomplished everything I could have at Ferro and there was very little room for upward mobility.

Throughout my career, I worked for three companies in a variety of HR roles before launching Careerminds. We've already discussed my lengthy time as an HR professional on the ground. Over those years, I vacuumed up all of the HR experience I could until I felt like I just couldn't improve anymore. I had reached a level that couldn't be passed by merely working in the roles I had been pursuing.

This time came during my fifth year working at Ferro. It was the beginning of 2006. At this point, I knew my days were numbered. Every day I went into work, I would sit at my desk and wonder about starting my own company and what that would look like. I had so many ideas but really struggled with how to get started. It just seemed so difficult to get going because there were so many things that I felt I needed to do.

Then, another career move was proposed. Toward the end of 2006, I had a performance review with my boss, JC Gibson, where he shared that the next upward step for me was to move to Cleveland, Ohio, where the corporate headquarters was located. The thought of moving again after just settling down in a new home, with a new spouse and a new baby, was not even the least bit appealing.

The idea of growing to the next level was exciting and flattering, but if I moved to Cleveland, I would be going alone. Abby said to me, "Why don't you start your new business? I'm stable now with my company and have medical benefits, so it won't be as much of a strain for the first few years." In the back of my mind I was thinking, can I really do it? What if I fail, or what if it doesn't work out?

Carol Dweck, the pioneering researcher on mindset, would probably not have been happy with my questioning but may advise that it was completely normal. According to Dweck's book, the questions I was asking myself, such as, "Can I really do it?" are characteristics of a fixed mindset. In other words, my talents and experiences are fixed and can't be developed, therefore I can't do it. It's a self-fulfilling prophecy. In contrast, in a growth mindset, my abilities and intelligence can be developed with effort, learning, and persistence. The growth minded question would have been, "How do I do it?"

This uncertainty I was having clearly stemmed from having more of a fixed mindset. People often get trapped in this mindset, particularly if they are afraid of taking risks or fear being judged or humiliated. What I learned is that I had the power of choice to change my thinking to be in more of a growth mindset, one that I could develop through dedication and hard work. With this belief, I had the power to learn and embrace the challenges I faced and persevere when setbacks invariably arose during the learning process.

Deep down inside I felt like it was time to take the risk and launch Careerminds, but I was still nervous and unsure of how to really get started. In the meantime, I spent some time looking at a few franchises, such as a UPS Store. A franchise would be a much easier starting point to get my feet wet because the brand was much more established and the likelihood for success would be much greater. I didn't want to fail with Careerminds, so I thought a franchise would be a good way to start first, then I could do Careerminds second.

However, that just seemed too complicated, and besides, I wasn't all that passionate about shipping packages every day. In fact, thinking back, this was still me being stuck in a fixed mindset. Instead of going after my true passion and obtaining what I really wanted, I put a roadblock in the way. I had no experience with shipping, just like I had no experience running an HR start-up, but—for some reason—the idea of UPS seemed easier when, in fact, it was just getting in the way. I'm very glad I ignored this type of thinking.

Toward the end of 2006, I realized that the timing was getting near and that if I was going to start Careerminds, I needed to make the decision by the end of the year. In January, I would get my bonus and my vacation would reset, so it would be the perfect time to share my desire to leave Ferro and begin plans to transition. So in January of the new year, I went to my boss, JC, and the head of HR to share my desire to start my own company.

They asked all of the normal questions one does: "What are you planning to do?" I told them that I was leaving the HR function and Ferro and starting a new company. The company name would be Careerminds. When I shared Careerminds, I could sense some skepticism in their voice, as if they'd heard this song and story before, just from different employees. I mentioned that I'd long wanted to be an entrepreneur and start something from scratch. Despite their lackluster reaction, I felt like being transparent with my intentions to start Careerminds was the right thing to do. Plus, I had another plan for my boss a bit later to present my transition out of the company that I wanted support on, so I needed them to support me on this venture.

The company asked me to think it over and come back to them with a definite decision after a few days. I was a great employee and one of their favorite HR managers, so they gave me the space I needed to make a final decision. Over the next few days, I weighed my options. It boiled down to three choices:

- Stay with Ferro and remain comfortable with an okay salary, okay benefits, and nice coworkers. Basically, easy but not fulfilling work.

- Find another HR job that was more fulfilling. This was a risky option because I could definitely find another job but end up right where I was then, just three to five years down the road, causing the cycle to continue.

- Start Careerminds! This was by far the scariest option. What made this option the scariest was that I could not picture the outcome. The thought of the unknown and not knowing what was in store made this option the toughest to choose, but I knew it was truly my only option.

So, after days of deliberation and thinking it through, I went back to my boss and told him that I was definitely leaving Ferro and starting a new chapter in my life. The next big pitch to my boss, after communicating that I was leaving the company, was for him to allow me to recruit, hire, and train my replacement so I'd have a transition that would allow me time to get Careerminds off the ground.

After all, I was starting Careerminds, a new recruiting company. I should at least be able to recruit my replacement. I wasn't going to dare ask for a placement fee, but the idea of Ferro becoming my first client did cross my mind; however, I needed to prove myself with this first hire. My boss agreed to allow me to find my replacement, and in February 2007, I became a contractor with Ferro and set off to find my HR replacement while supporting my facility on a part-time contract basis.

After a few months, I recruited and hired my replacement and the transition to Careerminds was well underway. During this time, the economy was doing really well and Ferro was in growth mode, so the company had lots of job openings across the country. As I wrapped up the transition of onboarding my replacement in the summer of 2007, I then approached the head of HR with a recruiting proposal and asked if she'd be okay if I reached out to my former HR colleagues with Ferro at other facilities around the company and ask for recruiting work. She respected me (and quite frankly, liked me), so she was very supportive of the request; however, they were not going to make it easy for me by reaching out and asking the HR community to use my services.

I had to, one-by-one, reach out and sell myself. It wasn't easy because the market was flooded with recruiters and Ferro had a long history of using really good ones. Out of the dozens of facilities across the country, I was only able to contract three locations who had a few job openings. The idea that I was going to be Ferro's exclusive new recruitment firm was far from being a reality. The challenges of building a new recruiting business seemed to become more and more realistic every day.

The other big challenge that became apparent very quickly was the insecurity I felt with my new founder and CEO title that I had taken on overnight. Just like that, I went from an HR manager of a small non-union plant in South Jersey to entrepreneur, founder and CEO of Careerminds, a national recruiting firm with one new account—my former company. I recall distinctly how I felt when I started Careerminds, printed my business cards, and started communicating my new CEO title to the world. It was like starting a new job with a new flashy job title. Let's just say, the title of founder and CEO didn't roll off my tongue as eloquently as it did for Mark Zuckerberg.

I remember feeling embarrassed saying I was the CEO of my company. I felt like I needed to prove it first before earning the title. I pressed on, though, and worked hard getting past those uncomfortable feelings. In the first year, I worked out of my home office, building out the website, marketing materials, and legal documents to make Careerminds official.

Working out of the house was difficult for me, particularly after spending 15 years in the corporate world. I was used to leaving the house every morning for an office. This new work routine was not comfortable in the least. So, I decided I needed an office to call my own. To that end, I found a friendly neighbor, Ray Tetlow, who was launching his second company and was searching for an office-mate. Ray was an eccentric, rough around the edges Brit from Manchester, England, who was brash but super smart and wildly successful. Ray would end up being a great friend and mentor for me and my new business. I would never tell him that, by the way, as his ego is nauseating.

I moved into my new office in Hockessin, Delaware, in the fall of 2007 and the recruiting business was starting to get some traction. Over the first nine months, I was able to make several new placements within facilities, obtain a couple of HR consulting gigs, as well as secure a few new outside recruiting assignments with other chemical companies. I'll never forget the day I received my first check. I still have it today. It was a shared placement that I did with another recruiter I met while working at Ferro.

My office-mate, Ray, was also supporting the growth of Careerminds as he introduced me to one of his clients, TheatreExtreme (TX), a fast-growing home entertainment company that was exploding with the housing boom. TX was heavily funded by Circuit City, as they were hiring sales managers for several new locations that were part of the Circuit City retail chain. With this new contract, I was feeling really great about year one.

The office environment was also really working out as I had a free resource in Ray to bounce things off of when I had some key decisions to make, one of which was when to add some new team members to help with the workload.

In early 2008, I found someone in Philadelphia who was willing to work as a sales rep for nearly 100 percent commission, as well as a young, fresh out of college recruiter who was willing to get paid when she placed candidates in jobs. Cash flow for a start-up is one of the biggest issues you'll deal with as an entrepreneur. By the way, I wasn't paying myself much of anything at this time, so everything I made went to the business and getting things going.

By this point, I was starting to get a bit comfortable with the start of the business. I had several clients, two employees willing to work for commission, and some steady income coming in on the placements we were making. We had a long way to go, but I wasn't feeling like I had to eat ramen noodles every day. One issue I struggled with was I wasn't all that passionate about recruiting. Recruiting was always a function of my role in HR, but the thought of doing this for the rest of my life as a business was not exactly what I felt like I was called to do, but I pressed on.

Little did I know at the time, but the next phase of my journey would present itself sooner than I anticipated.

Tip for Clocking Out

"Becoming a CEO of your own company is far easier than becoming a CEO of a company owned by another; however, it's much harder to sustain without the right recipe." The success of a CEO in a start-up comes with a good business plan, discipline, the drive and passion to succeed, willingness to pivot when things aren't working out, and the required start-up funds.

Donna Elliston:
A Passion for the Public

"Communities and countries and ultimately the world are only as strong as the health of their women."

—Michelle Obama

Mindset is one of the hardest principles to achieve. There are a ton of different concerns that can pop up that can drive a growth mindset right into a holding pattern. Should I keep progressing my career or should I take a step back right now? Maybe my next step should be a lateral one where I won't take on the full weight of my dream. These are just a few examples.

Taking risks is an extremely challenging thing to do. We all have goals and dreams, but most of the time it requires a trust in the process and one's self to achieve those goals and take the needed steps to remain in a growth mindset. This is where Donna Elliston comes in.

When I interviewed Donna, I could tell right away that she was the prime example of a growth mindset. From her early, early days she had a goal to help women and children in a medical capacity. Over the course of her career, she stayed on target and kept climbing higher and higher. Using agility to make tough choices along the way, Donna was able to achieve her dreams and stay focused the whole time. Here's how it happened.

Donna is a born and raised New Yorker who grew up in the Upper East Side. Her parents were instrumental in her aspirations. Her dad was a doorman for co-ops in the city and her mother was a retired registered nurse who worked the role for 35 years.

She attended Catholic school and an all-girls private school in Manhattan. From there, she went to Vassar College for her undergrad studies, where she studied sociology and was a pre-med major. She told me that this experience was great. It was the first time she was able to leave home and be on her own. She was excited to explore and get out into the world.

She also told me that growing up in New York City was a great experience. Her parents made it a point to expose her to all of the arts, movies, and culture that the city had to offer. She says that she still loves the city after all of this time, which is something that I find incredibly interesting as someone who loves to visit New York but also gets excited when it's time to leave.

Her early experience is also what led her to pre-med in college. She recalls always wanting to be a pediatrician. Her mom, after all, was a registered nurse, and she was always interested in child health, motherhood, and babies. She remembers going and playing with kids at hospitals. This moment, for her, was monumental in developing where her career would go even though it was so long ago.

At Vassar, students were allowed to elect fieldwork opportunities. She got to experience the medical world firsthand at a local Planned Parenthood clinic where she gained real responsibility with patients in the field. She loved it.

She graduated from Vassar with a degree in sociology (after switching from a bio major and taking all of the pre-med classes she could). Sociology was a great option for her because she started to focus on health care for populations instead of individuals. She loved learning about public health and how communities and populations impact health on a much grander scale.

After graduating, she returned to New York City and landed her first job, which was an interesting one. The role was basically a fact-checker position where reporters would call in and ask for, say, the rate of HIV spread and Donna and her colleagues would have to find an expert and verify the fact. They worked under a deadline and had to be pretty quick on their feet with an answer.

In today's world, this seems like something that would take seconds on Google, and that's true, but this was back in the late-80s before search engines were even an idea. Back then, she had to call scientists and experts to get the right information and then match those people with the reporters. She says that this was her first foray into research.

Eventually, though, it became time to leave after two years at the company. Part of the decision to accept this position and move back to the city was because her father passed away during her senior year at Vassar. She recalls her mother saying that her father would want her to finish what she started at school, so with the support of her college classmates who attended her dad's funeral, she immediately returned to Vassar on schedule to complete her senior year. It was a devastating time, but she stuck through it. Once school was finished, she knew she wanted to be close to her family for at least a year and returned home.

These decisions are rarely talked about when we discuss work and careers, but Donna is exemplifying a growth mindset and also a lot of agility. She made a plan and stuck to it, but also allowed herself to be there for her mother and family.

After she left the research job, she knew that she still wanted to be involved in medicine and that she needed to leave the city to venture outward. After jumping around a bit "figuring things out," she attended Meharry Medical College in Nashville where she took her first public health class. Her goal was to obtain a master's degree in the subject and she was excited to study at a historically black college and university.

It was here where she found out that public health was her true passion. Everything clicked at this moment. She always knew she wanted to be a doctor but now she knew exactly what she wanted to study and how she was going to make that goal a reality.

As a graduate student Donna worked for another Planned Parenthood agency, where she got to see firsthand how public health works on the ground level. If you recall, she always loved working with moms and children back when she wasn't even in college. Then she studied sociology at Vassar. Now, at Meharry, she was able to see that she could basically combine all of these into one degree and really make the difference she wanted to.

This is a great time to point out Donna's growth mindset. Over the course of her education, she knowingly—and sometimes unknowingly—was working towards a huge goal: becoming a doctor. It takes years and years to pull this off and Donna maintained that mindset over that entire time. She also had to be very agile with her choices.

Though she wanted to stay at Meharry, she knew that she'd have to leave if she wanted to continue her education and become a full-blown doctor. So, after obtaining her master of science degree in public health, she attended Morgan State University on a full scholarship. She was able to further her public health career at the doctoral level and transfer some of the course credits that she completed at Meharry. Because of all of this, she managed to obtain her Doctorate in Public Health (DrPH) degree as an applied researcher in just three and a half years. Typically, doctoral programs can take between four and seven years depending on a slew of different reasons, mainly because of dissertations.

For Donna, she decided to focus her dissertation on intimate partner violence during pregnancy, looking specifically to see whether black women were more at risk. She even got paired with a wonderful researcher from the Johns Hopkins University School of Public Health, who had a ton of data on the topic and granted permission for the use of her data for secondary data analysis, while mentoring Donna through the dissertation process, which helped her earn her degree faster.

After she graduated, she moved to Tampa and did a post-doc with an NIH researcher at the University of South Florida in St. Petersburg. She worked there for about two years before moving to Atlanta.

For those unfamiliar with public health as a career path, for most—including Donna—the end goal is to work for the Centers for Disease Control and Prevention (CDC), which is headquartered in Atlanta.

This was another moment where Donna was in an active growth mindset. During her post-doc, she knew that she wanted to eventually work for the CDC, but how was she supposed to pull that off? One of the first steps for her was to actually relocate to the city where they are and establish herself there.

Once in Atlanta, she didn't immediately land a CDC role. Instead, she worked for Jane Fonda's non-profit, which is now called the Georgia Campaign for Adolescent Power & Potential (GCAPP). The organization focuses on teen pregnancy prevention and adolescent health.

This was her very first job in Atlanta. She says that most of her roles came from networking and being in the right place at the right time, which is something that we hear at Careerminds quite often. For GCAPP, she attended a conference where she was introduced to the president and CEO of the organization. They hit it off and she was hired as an evaluation manager.

She says that this was an amazing experience and that GCAPP continues to do amazing things even to this day.

She was there for about a year before actually landing a role in the CDC with an Oak Ridge Institute for Science and Education (ORISE) fellowship that allowed people to work with top-tier scientists. She was involved with the adolescent reproductive health team where she learned how to pull off systematic reviews and analyze data and research. This was around 2007 or so, just to give you a timeline.

While working there, Donna says that it was very exciting. As an ORISE fellow, she was able to work with other new grads who were all in the same boat as her. She says the agency ran like a well-oiled machine with meetings, deadlines, and projects. This taught her a discipline within public health research, especially knowing that the whole world is looking at what the CDC says and does.

After her year as an ORISE fellow, she left the CDC to work in the private sector as a public health consultant. These organizations are basically government contractors where firms compete for proposals that the CDC and other federal agencies put out for them to bid on. This role was very, very fast-paced. Donna says that this was very much like the corporate world where the competition was fierce and, at times, cutthroat. It was a different experience than agency life. During this time in her career, she'd already managed to work for a non-profit, a government agency, and a more corporate role, rounding out just about every type of work you can do.

Consultant roles weren't really fulfilling for her, though. So she eventually went back to GCAPP to provide technical assistance to other community initiatives. Donna oversaw every step of this process. At first, she was skeptical if she could perform the role, but took it on anyway and quickly adapted.

Donna says that this is the turning point in her career. This was the first role where she was in a senior position. At this point, she had "made it," feeling like she was no longer a young, green public health worker. She was now in charge and was able to pull off the role.

Donna's growth mindset allowed her to continue pushing her career. Through agile moves and an inherent trust in the process (networking, fellowships, and more) she was able to move up the ladder with every transition. Each time she moved, she learned a little more and became more confident in herself and her abilities. Landing the senior role at GCAPP was a milestone. It was a culmination of everything she had done in the past going all of the way back to her first time working with Planned Parenthood during her undergrad.

Donna had worked at GCAPP for about four years when she knew the project was winding down. One of her previous bosses reached out to her from a consulting firm she worked at. This was another senior role and she quickly took up the offer to work for them. While there, she was able to mentor and manage staff, which is something she loves.

One thing that I find interesting about all of this is that public health is a very project-based career. Imagine working for a huge agency but only having a guaranteed position if funding is available. You need to be incredibly flexible and agile to find new opportunities every couple of years. This type of work is typical of doctorate researchers who leave academia. To me, it sounds stressful, but some people thrive doing it.

When I told this to Donna, she said that people typically work roles for three to five years on average. There are no really long, cushy careers at single companies for this type of work. You're always on the edge of being laid off because funds can quickly dry up or programs can end.

Donna also says that this is where it is important to have transferable skills because you will have to reinvent yourself quite often—definitely a lot more often than you would with traditional careers.

The entrepreneurial side of Donna emerged because of this way of working. Surely there are a ton of people who have been laid off because of these types of issues, but is there anyone out there that specifically focuses on public health researchers who need to find new work because their funding ran out?

Donna figured that she was a perfect person to fill that void. She says that this is in no offense to HR leaders and recruiters who are great at finding more traditional jobs, but when it comes to high-level researchers who have complicated—and oftentimes very long—CVs, you need someone who understands that world if you want to be successful landing a new role in a new firm.

Donna decided to create a company, named Public Health Solutions Executive Search Firm (PHS), that would allow firms to search for public health workers through a database where people can recommend candidates for roles or simply search through it to find the right person.

Basically, the company was created to fill a gap that was greatly needed for these workers. To pull this off, Donna talked it over with her current employer to make sure that she was legally allowed to work on her database while still being employed. They said that there was no conflict of interest, so Donna was free to pull in an income while building her business.

Again, this a great example of a growth mindset. She was able to work on her own project while also maintaining her current role. She was always looking at the future, setting goals, and making choices to meet those goals in the future. Founding her company came from the experience of working for many different places and coming up with a solution that she, herself, wished she had when she was looking for work after grants ran out and positions were let go.

Donna says that she even talks about agility during her coaching sessions with PHS, saying that it is important to not silo oneself. For example, she specializes in one specific area of public health, but she can transfer a lot of those skills and reinvent herself when needed. This is a skill set that is almost mandatory for those working in these types of roles.

Though Donna was making progress on her own business, she was eventually laid off from her full-time role. This is how I met Donna. Her firm hired Careerminds to give the staff assistance during their transitions. She says that this is one of the only times she's been provided with resources to help get through a job loss. She also liked that she had a coach this time, which is something she's usually on the other side of.

After working with her coach, she landed another consultant role that allowed her to focus more on PHS. She says that she's been very lucky to have had this road map in front of her where every step of the process was a move forward and that every future opportunity is better than the last. If that doesn't scream a growth mindset, I don't know what does. Donna says that everyone should follow their passion because "Your passion will lead to your purpose and your purpose will make room for what you will do professionally."

Donna says that public health is her passion. It's what she was put on this Earth to do, and she will do that no matter what. She won't chase money or titles. She wants to be a public health expert and help others in that community (plus all of the people that benefit from public health across the country and the world).

I hope I can keep up with everything Donna does next. She's always looking at the horizon and attempting to reach it.

Tip for Clocking Out

"Your passion will lead to your purpose and your purpose will make room for what you will do professionally." Through this mindset, Donna was able to stay focused, plan for her career, make agile changes, and create the exact career she set out to. Throughout all of this, she shows that mindset goes an incredibly long way and helps all of the other principles outlined in this book come together.

Dana Vogelmeier:
All According to Plan

"Success is the sum of small efforts,
repeated day in and day out."

—Robert Collier

Mindset comes in all different shapes and sizes. For some, it's the ability to keep on track while making agile choices. For others, it involves careful planning and sticking to a process. Trust often times plays a big role in this type of mindset because one has to truly trust themselves and the process that they've created.

Dana Vogelmeier definitely falls into the latter category. Throughout her life, she looked at the future, was able to understand how her choices today impacted that future, and then made steps to ensure she would stay on the right track.

Still, I cannot state it enough that a growth mindset is the result of many other principles. For example, you have to be agile in order to keep on track with your goals, you have to trust the process or you will abandon it long before you see results, and lastly, you need to make choices. In fact, making choices is a core aspect of all of the principles.

Dana grew up in Central Ohio, living just outside of Columbus. When she was 16 her family moved to a suburb of Columbus where she attended a much bigger school than she was used to. You could say this was her very first career transition, happening at a very early age.

She was the youngest of three girls. She lived with her single mom and visited her father on the weekends. Recalling her younger days, Dana said her sisters were really close in age—about a year apart—and her sisters were six and seven years older than her. She says that this meant that she was pretty much an only child after her sisters left the house. This age gap was strange but Dana said the shift to just her in the house was a quiet one. Though it was just her and her mom most of the time, there were good and bad things about this.

From her perspective, her mother's hard work rubbed off on her. Her mother was very independent and worked to support Dana and her sisters as an executive secretary. Her father worked at the airport as a ticketing agent. Dana's mother worked in the evenings to make ends meet. All of this impacted Dana at a very early age and she says it is why she is so hardworking today.

Dana's very first job was in the small town she grew up in as a waitress in a family diner. She says it was nothing fancy but she worked with other kids from her high school, who made up most of the staff there.

Even though this was many years ago, Dana still remembers how regimented the restaurant was. At certain times, certain things happened. For example, at a specific time, everyone would wrap silverware and things like that. She fondly remembers the camaraderie of working there, having fun, and being on the same page as everyone else. It was like working inside a well-oiled machine that depended on teamwork, an aspect of the job she still loves to this day.

This was all when she was around 15. The next year, she made the big move to her new school and took up a job at McDonald's, a proving ground for many teenagers to this day. Dana said that this move was challenging because it was just far enough to require her to find a new friend group late into her high school life.

Dana says that the move to "the big city" was a pivotal point in her life because it broke her small-town mentality. She learned that there were a lot of opportunities out there and it also helped her adapt to a new environment quickly, a skill that everyone should have.

When graduation time came around, Dana had to figure out what her next step would be. Her family wasn't all that much into college. Her mother and father both didn't attend and neither did one of her sisters, though her oldest sister did. At the same time, people at her school were already taking classes at night while still in high school. This opened up Dana's mind to the possibility of continuing her education, though she was still unsure.

Eventually, after much deliberation, she decided to attend community college. This was back in 1982. Dana had a plan: she wanted to go to work for a place that would reimburse her tuition. However, there were only two places that she could work at for this to happen.

With this goal in mind, she obtained her associate's degree and transferred to Franklin University in downtown Columbus, which enabled her to be eligible for the reimbursement. She then started to apply to both of these organizations. One of them was Bank One—which no longer exists—and the other was State Farm.

Dana applied and applied and applied. Finally, State Farm called and offered her a very, very entry-level position as a file clerk paying her about five dollars per hour. She was 19 at this point, and landed the role she wanted for State Farm to pay for college tuition. It took her a few years to get her degree in business management, but she managed to get out debt-free.

What's funny is that Dana actually met her husband at school in one of her classes. He was actually working for Bank One, pulling off the very same strategy she was. It was a coincidence that eventually pulled them together, and they married soon after.

This early on, you can already see Dana being extremely agile and having a great mindset. She saw an opportunity to get schooling paid for and even obtained a master's degree later down the road in leadership all by observing her options and making quick moves to better herself. At the same time, she trusted her own process and the process for tuition reimbursement that was laid out in front of her. Very few teenagers have this type of mindset. Usually, it takes a bunch of career moves to start thinking this way, but Dana (and her husband) were quite different.

So, now in her mid-twenties, Dana was working as a file clerk as she obtained her four-year degree. In the early days, she applied to move up from being a file clerk and was actually able to move out of the position and into a higher-level role in just about nine months. A year later, she moved up again. This was all still while she was getting her degree. Dana's careful to mention that these roles, though higher than when she started, were still very much entry-level. She still had to punch a clock, for example.

In order to truly move up the ranks, she had to wait until she fully obtained her degree since that was required for furthering her along in the company.

Her first truly professional role inside the company was as an underwriter. Then, she continued along this path and applied to a new role in Cleveland because her husband was accepted to law school there, a dream he always wanted to fulfill. A few years later, she moved again back to Central Ohio as an underwriter.

If you're confused by this all, fear not! During this time, Dana was trusting the corporate process by performing her job well and continued moving up the ranks. The move, which lasted three years, shows just how well she was doing at the company. It is, after all, a lot to ask to move across the state and continue at the same organization, then to move back and still work there. You typically only hear of this happening in extremely large tech companies like Google, which allow employees to be almost nomadic as long as they get their work done.

Around 1996, they came back to Central Ohio. During this time, the office was still only open until five in the afternoon, but they were going to offer a pilot program where customers could still be served after five. They asked who would want to work longer hours on weekends and until nine at night. Very few people wanted to take up this role, but Dana decided to give the pilot a try and take one for the team.

This pilot was only supposed to last nine months, but there was an absolute ton of demand and the program took off. Slowly, Dana started to have a leadership role for this pilot program because more and more staff members were required to pull it off. Among other tasks, she created policies and documentation to help the system run. Dana performed this "nine-month pilot" for about a year and a half before another opportunity struck.

Because of her success, she was asked to move to the company's headquarters in Bloomington, Illinois, a place two hours south of Chicago and six hours west of where she currently lived.

At this point in her life, in around 1996, Dana had a three-year-old daughter and her husband was working as an attorney, but he was not allowed to practice law in Illinois. Instead, he worked for an organization in Dallas, Texas, coming home on the weekends. This only lasted a year until a new gig came around for him back in Illinois to help a collections agency with their legal matters, a role that would open a door very shortly for the family to move yet again.

When Dana moved into corporate, she eventually worked her way up into a manager role, achieving her first leadership position. She worked this role for three years before Texas came calling again.

In 2000, Dana got the chance to become an assistant director at a bilingual call center in El Paso. The family packed up and moved yet again. This time, her husband was able to launch his own practice based on the collections experience he had gained back in Illinois.

During her time in Texas, Dana was able to build the call center from the ground up, literally. The building was brand new and it needed to be staffed and managed, a role that Dana was happy to carry out. While there, she also obtained a master's degree in leadership from the same university back in Ohio, performing her scholarly duties remotely while working. State Farm, again, paid for her tuition. This time, her degree directly increased her ability to perform her job.

One of the biggest issues to arise during this time working with State Farm was Hurricane Katrina. The magnitude of the event on the call center was absolutely insane. Dana says she remembers having to deal with a way higher frequency of calls and even seeing her call center employees break down and start crying on the phone based on what the customers were saying from New Orleans. She says that this was one of the realest moments of her career. She's proud that she was able to help so many people through it. It was a time at the call center she'll never forget.

A few years later, around 2007 or so, she switched from the insurance side of State Farm to the banking side, running a call center over there until around 2011—the same year her daughter graduated high school.

Guess what happened next? Another move, this time back to corporate. After 11 years in Texas, she was uprooted yet again. This time, though, her husband was actually able to land a role inside the company, too, making the move back easier than the ones previously, though it was still a shock to the system after carving out a life near the border.

As luck would have it, her daughter applied and was accepted to Ohio State. The whole family now had a reason to head back north.

Dana's new role was as "dean," which is a position that basically oversees the learning that the organization does. One of her tasks, for example, was to create high-performing environments and help the department improve the workplace. This is where she found her calling and it's what she does today for other companies. It was an interesting role that you typically don't hear about all too often in the corporate world. It was sort of aligned with HR and its mission to increase culture inside the organization.

A few more moves and five years later, she eventually landed in the role of learning and development, which was a logical step from her previous roles. Leading up to this role, she knew she wanted to get out of the bank role. She knew she wanted to leave at age 55 in 2019, too, which meant that she had a view of what she wanted to see on the horizon.

Working in L&D, she was able to work on and develop multiple areas of the business instead of being siloed in the banking section. Her title during this time was Senior Learning Manager, reporting to the directors of learning. Despite L&D seeming very HR-focused, the department was completely different and had their own chain of command up the corporate ladder to the VPs.

Dana says that leading these teams was great for her because it enabled her to learn more and more and get ready for her future. If you couldn't tell, Dana is extremely good at looking ahead and planning accordingly, going all the way back to her college days.

This same mindset came to a head again around 2016. At this time, both Dana and her husband were starting to feel like they weren't truly challenged anymore. Also, Dana had envisioned leaving the organization in 2019 at age 55. The two of them started planning. As you may recall, both of them had the same college plan, and it was like they were bookending their careers the same way they started: with an iron-clad plan of attack. They even downsized their house so that they could make the future move. At this point, they knew they were going to leave their jobs, but they still didn't really know what they intended to do with their newfound free time.

Unfortunately, like the best-laid plans of mice and men, things fell apart. In August 2018, word of restructuring started to be heard echoing through the halls of the organization. Around the same time, her husband was contacted by another company to fulfill an open position that they had. Things, to put it simply, were starting to impede on the plan.

Her husband ended up moving to Columbus for the new role toward the end of 2017. Dana was at this point waiting it out to see if a potential reduction in force (RIF) event was going to impact her role. If it wasn't, she would resign.

The stars started to align, though. She eventually got word that there would be restructuring of the department and there were, indeed, going to be layoffs. As everything started to unfold, Dana was excited to learn that she could take a voluntary severance package. The company still gave her quite a while to think everything over and even let her apply for other roles inside the organization.

Dana jumped on the voluntary package, knowing that she wanted to exit anyway and start her own thing, whatever that would be at this point. This meant, though, that she had to stay until the end in August 2018, which was her last date at the company she worked at for over 33 years of her life.

Just to put her planning into perspective here, Dana wanted to leave the organization in May 2019. The stars aligned, as she put it, but the company still cut her timeline short just a bit. One of the most challenging things about this part of her career was helping her other staff members navigate the transition. Needless to say, especially if you've read the other stories in this book so far, layoffs are incredibly stressful. Dana started putting the emotional needs of others in front of her own, helping them get through all of this even though she was excited about her personal move.

Still, people all around her felt shell-shocked. People had worked for the company for years and years. The sudden shift was a big issue, one that typically didn't happen at State Farm, a company that doesn't have restructuring events or layoffs all that often. In other words, people weren't expecting to lose their jobs.

Dana learned that she had to support those individuals, listen to their issues, and try to be there for them as much as she could. She was surprised at the different levels of emotion and anger from different people. Some were immediately sad, some were shocked but not angry, some were positive. It was a wild ride.

She reports that some people actually used the severance to do things that they really wanted to do that they never did. For example, one person became a realtor and loved it. Another retired and started studying photography. Still, there were a lot of people who needed support landing more traditional roles.

What I find interesting in this whole ordeal is that the entire department—we're talking hundreds of people—came together and really rooted for each other to succeed. They gave each other reports and checked in; it was a village coming together in their mutual time of need.

Back to Dana. It's August of 2018. She is finally, truly out of State Farm after over 33 years. What was she going to do now?

Dana always wanted to work for herself and, starting way back in 2016, she started helping companies with their leadership and development initiatives under the banner of Vogelmeier Consulting. Dana wasted no time jumping into her new job, joining chambers of commerce, the Rotary Club, the National Association of Women Business Owners, and many other organizations.

Dana truly was off to the races with her consulting work, moving from networking to subcontracting work. She currently teaches a bunch of different skill sets at various institutions, a role that was very much like her old L&D and "dean" positions. She also teaches part-time for the Association for Talent Development (ATD), a task that she really loves to perform.

Dana was in full growth mindset mode, pushing herself and her new business further and further into the future even after technically retiring with a voluntary severance package. Her husband landed another role in Columbus as well, allowing them even more financial freedom.

Now, Dana is able to work with many different organizations and use her experience to help others, which she loves. She currently does this role full-time, though she is still trying to figure out her full-time schedule. She's also still working with various independent rotary clubs and organizations with similar purposes. She says that she's always wanted to reach higher levels in these organizations and now she has the chance to help out with these humanitarian issues with other business leaders.

Dana says that she still loves working independently for corporations, but she doesn't miss the corporate environment and would rather keep doing what she's doing now instead of rejoining the traditional workforce. In her words, she's busy. Too busy for that lifestyle on top of the one she's developed for herself post–State Farm.

Dana's story is unique in this collection because she was uniquely set up to deal with her role being restructured. She used it as a springboard to do what she truly wanted: work for herself. She was able to do all of this because she continued to have a growth mindset that allowed her to make agile choices and trust the process she created for herself.

She recommends that others start to make networks early on in their careers and continue to foster relationships because those who do typically have a much better time transitioning their careers. She also notes that people should continually develop their skills to keep themselves employable long into the future.

Tip for Clocking Out

"Plan, plan, plan." Dana's mindset is all about having a concrete plan and then the trust to adhere to that plan. Starting out, she even managed to find a way to pay for college and then leveraged that role into her future success. Throughout the twists and turns of her career, she always looked forward and maintained a growth mindset that is rarely seen. Plans can fall apart, which happened to her on a few occasions, but with the right mindset she was able to make and adjust her plan to always be marching forward.

8

Career-minded:
Agility, The Pivot

"It's not the strongest of the species that survive, nor the
most intelligent, but the one most responsive to change."

—Charles Darwin

When founded, Careerminds was trying to take advantage of a booming housing market and a strong economy in 2008 as companies around the country struggled with attracting top talent.

As a new entrepreneur, I was trying to find my identity in the market. I still struggled with saying who we were and what we did. I felt like I was trying to be everything to everyone. I was recruiting, consulting, and anything else I could do to push the company as a whole forward. Although I felt busy, I didn't really feel like I was completely happy with what I was creating; however, I kept going.

Then, like most of this story, something outside of my control happened seemingly overnight.

On September 15, 2008, Lehman Brothers filed for bankruptcy and the beginning of the financial crisis and housing crash popped up on the horizon. At the time, I had no appreciation of how this change in the economy would impact Careerminds, but it became painfully apparent in the coming days.

Up until this point, Ferro was my largest account, as I had several open job requisitions that my recruiter was working on. We had a flat-screen Vizio TV in the Hockessin office, and Ray and I watched CNBC each day as the stock market crumbled and bank after bank filed for bankruptcy. I was sitting at my desk when an email hit my inbox from my good friend Herb Hingley, a plant manager with Ferro. The email was a forward from then Ferro CEO, Jim Kirsch, with a company-wide email communication that said: "Effective immediately, all open job requisitions will be on hold until further notice." Of course, this was a reaction to the stock market and financial crash as CEOs and organizations weren't really sure what to make of it all. Their first instinct, pretty much across the board, was to hit the pause button on everything, especially recruiting.

After reading that email, a knot formed in my stomach and I began to sweat nervously. I looked over in the office next door and saw my recruiter sitting there reviewing resumes of candidates she was planning to send off to a client for review. She could see in my eyes that something was wrong. All of that work, all of those job openings, all of those resumes, gone! We lost our largest account, my former company, just like that.

After I gathered my thoughts, I said to myself that it would be fine. Ferro was really good to me, and I couldn't have expected them to be around forever. Besides, I had these new accounts and the fast-growing TX home entertainment business. There was much to be excited about with these new accounts that were promised to grow exponentially.

I can't specifically recall if it was later that day or later that week after I received the email announcement about the Ferro hiring freeze, but my office phone rang, and it was my contact at Theatre Xtreme, Justin Schakelman. Justin was the cofounder and Chief Learning Officer of TX. He was responsible for training the newly hired sales managers to work with the Circuit City stores. Justin was a showman who had an unusual sense of humor, but on that day when he called, I could hear it in his voice that he was calling with sad news.

Justin, in a cracked voice, said, "TX is going bankrupt." I was speechless. I knew how hard he worked to get to the point where he was with his company. He was successful at taking TX public and raising investment capital from the behemoth Circuit City. It was the perfect storm of scenarios, unfortunately. At exactly the same time, TX fell into bankruptcy alongside Circuit City, who was a big investor in TX.

With the bankruptcy of Circuit City, a lack of funding, and the housing crash, TX could not survive. Their corporate headquarters in Newark, Delaware, would be closed down and all of the employees would be terminated immediately. As much as I couldn't bear getting any more bad news about losing business, I couldn't help but think about all those employees with TX who would be losing their jobs during the holiday season of 2008. Being in HR and seeing the downsizings of the dot-com boom at Corning, I can clearly recall the stress that employees experience with a reduction in force. It is not fun.

I sat on the phone with Justin and just listened to him talk through the process of what was going to happen during the transition with TX. I was no longer on the phone with a client but was there as a friend to console him through what would be one of the toughest transitions he would face in his career, one that I must admit, I hoped I wouldn't ever experience. TX, after going public and receiving funding from Circuit City, was a multimillion-dollar business and now it was gone, overnight, along with Justin's wealth.

I felt so incredibly horrible for him and his coworkers. At the end of the call, Justin said to me, "By the way, I know you worked in HR for many years and have lots of experience with recruiting and helping people find jobs. Do you think you'd be interested in working with our employees by helping them with writing their resumes and navigating their job transitions?"

I said, "Do you mean 'outplacement?' The answer is 'YES!'" At that moment, the light bulb went on. Careerminds would "pivot" away from recruiting and become an outplacement company going forward.

This pivot wasn't a knee jerk reaction to a new bright shiny object, but to something that was a culmination of experience, market timing, and opportunity.

In a business context, agility is the ability of an organization to rapidly adapt to market and environmental changes. Careerminds was only in business for a year as a recruiting company, so the idea of pivoting and redefining ourselves was not an issue. Throughout careers and business, we need to be able to recognize when change is needed and be proactive to change when it occurs.

As I saw the opportunity, the market demanded better outplacement services and, after overseeing one at Corning, I knew I was the guy for the job.

The question would then become, what kind of an outplacement company do I want Careerminds to be? There were many questions I had about this new direction, but that wasn't important at that moment. We had a bunch of employees who were without a job that we needed to help transition to something new. That was priority number one at this point. Get those people back to work so that they could continue their lives.

I made a deal with Justin that I would personally help all 10 corporate employees transition for $1.00 each. I wanted to charge them something to make it a legitimate transaction, but in return, I would ask for a testimonial from the CEO of the company.

The challenge in delivering outplacement services for these few employees was that I didn't have the office space to support an in-person, face-to-face program for each of them. Also, with my experience at Corning and Talent2Talent outplacement, I recalled vividly how employees didn't use the offices all that much and quite often used their home office and the internet to conduct their job search, and that was back in 2001. We were now in 2009, a decade later. LinkedIn was founded in 2002 and was really taking off as the standard of online professional networking, and the profile of the modern-day job seeker and worker was quickly evolving.

The idea that people would have to get in a car to drive 45 minutes for a 30-minute interview preparation session would be a thing of the past. I have to admit, the idea of having to open offices around the United States or even the world was unimaginable, but the idea of building something innovative, like a software platform in the Cloud and hiring virtual career consultants to deliver the coaching over the phone and through email seemed like something I could accomplish fairly quickly. Plus, it seemed like this was how the industry was headed. With the global recession well underway in the early part of 2009, I knew time was of the essence.

Over the next week, the resumes of the TX employees started coming in and the coaching work with each of the employees started to occur. I was already impressed with Justin's background as the cofounder of TX, but when I received his resume to begin his outplacement program, I couldn't believe my eyes.

Justin not only was the cofounder of TX, but he held a PhD in educational technology from the University of Delaware and had a solid track record of building social learning systems for high-profile companies. Along with his education, he had experience with raising venture capital, which would be of great importance later in the journey. I knew after seeing his resume that he would be a valuable asset to getting this new outplacement operation off the ground.

In a short period of time, I struck a deal with Justin to join Careerminds as an employee and help build out what is today called our Career Management System (CMS), which houses our virtual outplacement delivery platform.

The mission of Careerminds was to reduce the stress that employees face from a job loss and transition. As we stated earlier, losing your job is a very stressful event to most, so the value proposition for Careerminds was focused on reducing that stress. One of the ways we did that was to remove time-bound limits on programs. For years, the industry structured programs to be time-bound.

In other words, if you were laid off, companies would purchase a one-month, three-month, or six-month program depending on the level of your role at the company. If you were an executive you may get a six-month program, or if you were an IT administrator, you may get a one- or three-month program. Much of the decisions were also based on budget. The problem with the time-bound program approach is if an employee was at the end of their program and were still interviewing, they would lose support before crossing the finish line and landing a new job. This would defeat the purpose of outplacement as job seekers need help with interviewing, salary negotiations, and so on.

Since we were leveraging technology and virtual delivery and didn't have the infrastructure cost, we could make our programs *"until placement"* so that participants wouldn't stress that support would end. The other factor was that the model could also be less expensive than the brick and mortar programs that exist today.

We were really excited about what we had and the possibility of building something great. The global recession proved to be the perfect opportunity to introduce a new way of outplacement to the market. During this time, thousands of companies were laying off employees—some of which had never been through a massive layoff before. In order for us to get our name out there, we partnered with independent HR consultants, executive coaches, and recruiters to sell our virtual outplacement to organizations that were looking for a better, faster, more affordable, modern-day way to deliver outplacement. Agile thinking was key to success, not only for anticipating what's ahead, but for moving quickly to capitalize on the opportunity and being willing to take a risk and act quickly.

Tip for Clocking Out

"Agile thinkers respond to change with action and movement." Are you an agile thinker? Some of the characteristics of agile thinking include being energetic, limber, lively, quick, rapid, and sharp. Research suggests that flexibility and a willingness to adapt are highly correlated to being agile. In other words, if you have high levels of career flexibility and are capable of leaning into change, you're more likely to be agile in your career versus not being flexible and sticking to a rigid plan.

9

Mike Herrera: $\vec{F}=m\vec{a}$

"*Mathematics is not about numbers,
equations, computations, or algorithms:
it is about understanding.*"

—William Paul Thurston

As you know from the other stories in this collection, agility can be used many different ways. For some, agility comes during times of adversity and, for others, agility is all about looking ahead at the future.

In this story, we'll examine another form; specifically, how agility is used to make changes in careers that just aren't fitting. This is true "clocking out." We've all worked jobs that we no longer felt engaged with or didn't see a future in, but how many of us have actually stopped working those jobs for greener pastures? How many of us trusted ourselves enough to pursue an opportunity even if we weren't 100 percent sure it was correct? Well, agility allows you to do this. You can change the chances and—if you're agile enough—learn from them even if they were missteps.

Agility is a tool and a mindset. It also requires a ton of trust in one's self and the process. This story showcases all of these aspects of agility.

Born in East L.A. to a police officer father and social worker mother, Mike Herrera was the second oldest after his brother. Mike's mother and father had a rocky relationship that eventually led to their divorce when Mike was young. I empathize with Mike as my parents split up at a similar age. He recalls spending time at his mother's place where he lived and that his dad, who worked as a police officer for a bit and then had a slew of other jobs working for the city, was always bouncing around careers.

In her second marriage, Mike's mother had two more children, giving Mike two other siblings that are 11 and 14 years younger than he is, quite a big age gap. While sometimes these groups of siblings born far apart can take on relationships outside of the norm, with the younger siblings really looking up to their older brother or sister as a second parent, Mike says that he wasn't all that close with his two half-siblings.

Instead, he said that he was a bookworm, a lover of science, and was pretty closed off, but he wouldn't call himself shy. Either way, his brother was the domineering one out of the two of them, so he believes they looked up to him quite a bit more.

I found this part of the story interesting because it reflects my similar experience that you read in the introduction. Almost too well, if you ask me. My parents, just like Mike's, married at a young age when they were still teenagers. They divorced when I was 8 (my younger brother was 7, the same age as Mike was). It's weird how the world works.

Back to Mike, he says that living in a big city like L.A. wasn't that big of a deal to him growing up. Most people stuck to their neighborhoods (East L.A. for Mike) and it was like a small village. One thing he does recall is the fact that he lived close to the East L.A. Interchange. For you non-L.A.-ers, it's possibly the most confusing and chaotic intersection in the world where the 5, the 101, the 60, and the 10 all merge together.

Growing up and going through school, Mike was drawn to physics. He dreamed about being in a physics lab one day when he got older. Math was a challenge at the beginning, he says, and that it wasn't until later on—around eighth grade or so—when algebra came into the mix. He even took a summer class to knock out Algebra II while outside of school.

He quickly progressed through other math courses, too, taking trigonometry in the mornings. This was when he was still in junior high, by the way! Mike was essentially in ninth grade taking high school junior-level math courses. He had no idea how his guidance counselor would figure all of this out.

He didn't stop there. Mike had a geometry teacher that let him read all about quantum theory and higher-level concepts. He was hooked. He knew he wanted to study physics and become a physicist.

This led him to apply to Caltech, which he eventually graduated from. No, he didn't end up doing physics, but he did major and graduate with a bachelor's in mathematics. I know those two sound like they are the same, but believe me, they are not, as any mathematician or physicist will tell you.

I asked Mike, tongue-in-cheek, if he finished college in two years or something super-fast. He replied that no, laughing, that he wasn't a super genius, though he did recall being astounded when he saw 15-year-old kids on campus studying the same thing he was. It was wild to know that some people out there were that accelerated at such an early age.

During his free time, Mike also taught and tutored kids, making some money on the side for food and stuff like that. He liked teaching quite a bit, loved to shape young minds. This was all swirling around in his head when he finally obtained his diploma.

So where does one go with a degree in mathematics back in the mid-to-late '90s? Mike says that there were really only two options:

academia or coding. Back then, the language of the day was C++. There weren't many other options.

For Mike, the choice was pretty clear. He liked teaching a lot, so logically, he became a public school teacher at Garfield High School in L.A., one of the most populated schools in L.A. County and his alma mater.

Mike worked as a teacher from 2000 to about 2003, he says. He also told me that part of his reasoning for working in such a big, chaotic inner-city school was to give back to kids who were a lot like himself. People with degrees from Caltech, Harvard, Stanford, and the like typically don't wind up in the public school system, but Mike chose to.

His goal was to find kids like he was back in school and mentor them, and he did. He managed to obtain a whole classroom full of them—40 to 45 kids per class. He said that being an inner-city school, the school had its inner-city problems. Kids had parole officers. Kids got pregnant extremely young. Still, he looked out for all of them and tried to impart as many life lessons as possible, paying special attention to those who really, really wanted to learn math.

"There were some kids who were in the algebra classes, who I found were really stars and I moved them forward as much as I could," he told me.

"So identifying those kids was great. If they were in a horrible period where everybody else in the class was just hard to manage and so they weren't gonna learn, I moved them to an earlier period in the day, in one of my other classes where they accelerated."

Though from the outside looking in this environment seemed hard to deal with, Mike says the real issue was the other teachers, not the students themselves. He had nothing but praise for every one of the students he mentioned. Many of the other teachers carried a negative outlook, and that really wore on Mike.

Teaching kids was great, but after a while teaching algebra gets old. He likens algebra to breathing. It's essential to progress in mathematics, but it's not the most exciting stuff. He did, for a while, teach calculus, but the kids who were in his class were smart enough to not really need his help. If he wanted to make a difference, he'd have to stick to algebra, a thought that didn't sit well with him.

Then, an opportunity came his way. He was talking to his girlfriend (who is now his wife) and she was asking him the hard questions: So what do you want to do? Do you want to go back to school? A few days later, she actually came across a graduate program offered by Claremont Graduate University. The degree: Financial Engineering.

"It basically is a lot of mathematics and probability, mixed into pricing derivatives. And at the time, that's who were the quants on Wall Street," explains Mike, better than I can.

"They were basically physicists, string theorists, mathematicians, computer scientists, astrophysicists who basically used math and science to solve most of the problems in finance and model them."

To make the transition, Mike left his job at the school and became an undergraduate admissions officer at Harvey Mudd, which—it just so happened—was right across the street from Claremont Graduate University. He ended up making a deal with his boss to allow him to perform his job duties but to also allow him to go to class whenever he needed to. His bosses accepted this as long as he'd get his work done.

Over the next couple of years—moving into 2005—Mike eventually graduated with his Master of Science in Financial Engineering, and had even transitioned from Harvey Mudd and into a role as assistant director of undergraduate admissions at Caltech. He also got married in 2005, too, to his longtime girlfriend.

Next, he was off to the races. An interview with Goldman Sachs propelled him across the country to New York City.

Let's pause right here and talk about all of these moves because they happened very quickly. Mike was working a fine job in the public school system, but he wasn't progressing the way he wanted to. This is a prime example of a growth mindset. He then made a bunch of agile choices in a row. He found a job working in admissions—so still in the education space—and used that role to obtain a graduate degree for a very in-demand field. Then, almost immediately after, he went to work for one of the biggest investment firms on the planet. In the course of five years, Mike was agile, made smart choices, retained a growth mindset, and trusted the process he set for himself.

So how did this position even fall into Mike's lap, I hear you wondering? Networking! While working at Caltech, Mike decided to go to one of the job fairs that the university was hosting. While there, he saw an old Caltech friend who happened to be working for Goldman Sachs. The two got to talking and Mike let him know that he was looking for a job and had just obtained his financial engineering degree. His friend snatched up the resume and the rest is history. Right place, right time, right people.

He remembers when he was interviewing on the phone for the position that the guy asking him questions didn't even talk about finance. Instead, it was all math questions, asking him to solve multiple high-level questions—such as solving non-homogeneous linear differential equations (yes, that is real)—while on the phone. Mike says he recalls holding the phone in one hand and scribbling the problems with the other. He must have gotten all of the answers right because they decided to fly him to the Big Apple the next week.

The interview was even more intense. He was surrounded by people asking him a bunch of extremely technical, high-level math questions and having him solve them on the fly with little time to think. His wife, who was his fiancée at the time, waited for him in a cafe for most of that time, eventually meeting up with a friend in the city. Could you imagine that?

Oh, and guess what? He had to do it all again the next day with a new group of interviewers. Still, Mike passed with flying colors and they offered him a job. Over the next weeks to a month, Mike and his fiancée had to find out where they were going to live in New York, eventually deciding to live in New Jersey and take the train into Manhattan.

Though Mike was a little afraid to start this new job—it was for one of the biggest firms in existence, after all—he says that his biggest shock ended up being experiencing seasons. He was an L.A. kid. He was not prepared for the harsh New York climate swings. Even the rain was a new experience, for the most part.

Another harsh reality: the aftermath of the September 11th attacks. Mike's train would leave him off at Ground Zero every day and he remembers, because this was back when Ground Zero was still an active working zone, people still getting pulled out of the rubble years after the attack.

"I'd ride the PATH Train every day to Ground Zero and during this time they were still doing construction on the new towers, but as they would dig and excavate, they would find people," he told me.

"So they would stop construction and then you would see investigators come in to then look at what's going on and pull people out."

This was also a shock to the system, to say the least. Mike was in L.A. working as a teacher when the attacks happened. Sure, everyone saw them on TV, but this was reality. It was eye-opening.

New York, in general, didn't agree with Mike. He didn't want to leave his wife all day and be a Wall Street guy who never saw his family. He didn't want his kids to grow up in the concrete jungle, but luckily he was good at his job, so he was able to talk to the company get them to allow him to relocate back to California and work out of the very same building *Die Hard* was filmed in. No, really, Goldman Sachs operates out of Nakatomi Towers (which is really called the Fox Plaza).

This all took place two years later, in 2007. Even after the move, the hours were insane and it just wasn't working out. Six months later, he found a new role in the L.A. area working as a supervisor for an asset management company where he could transfer the skills he obtained at Goldman, but he wasn't a developer or as much a part of the business.

This position also didn't really fulfill Mike. Sure, he was back in California and the job wasn't all that bad, but he started to miss the IT side of things that he did at Goldman. He wanted to be more involved. So, after four years, he made another move. This time, it was to a firm right down the street from the asset management company. He started there as a business analyst and later got moved to another group with even more responsibilities. Mike says that he was in mostly software roles as an engineer and then as an architect.

In particular, he was in charge of the warehouse data. He developed systems that were easy to read for everyone involved, which helped keep the entire business running in his own way. The other thing Mike loved about this position was that he was able to do many different things that really worked well in a small company.

Mike worked this role for seven years, finally finding a place he could settle into. That is, until the company had a reduction in force in 2019. The company, which consisted of about 100 people, reduced their workforce by 20 percent, eliminating 20 jobs. They gave everyone a week's notice. Mike initially thought that he was going to survive the cuts but, in the end, he didn't.

What was he to do now? He had grown comfortable in that role, which was great but also meant that he needed to really update his resume and learn how to sell himself again. Mike really struggled with his identity here because he was able to mold the perfect position that tapped into a bunch of different skill sets. People like Mike often fall into a trap of saying to companies, "I can do all kinds of things for you, because of my experience." As Mike thought about his next opportunity, he knew he wasn't going to find exactly what he had had because the position didn't really exist.

The company offered him outplacement support and he worked with Careerminds to hone his resume, cut the fat, and really figure out what he wanted to do next. He told me that he worked with a whopping 12 different recruiters who all *almost* got him various interviews, but none panned out. They didn't pan out because, again, he was looking for a position that didn't exist. It was crazy because you had a super smart job candidate who could solve any problem, but he couldn't crack the job search "code." His career coach said, "Mike, you have to define specifically what you want!"

He woke up one day, and said, "That's it, I want to work with data. I'm a data geek so I'm going to hone my resume and look for a data job, besides that's where the world is headed, analytics and managing big data."

After searching for a data position for a while, he ran into a Caltech friend. It turned out that he had applied to a position in his friend's company but never heard back, probably because he wasn't focused at the time. His friend told him to give him some time. After waiting a bit, he got an interview at that company and managed to land another role working with data, a passion of his.

The great thing about this story and job is that it was the data focus that got him the interview and the job, but once he got in there, the hiring manager learned of all the other things Mike would be able to contribute to the job and the company. It was a win-win situation.

"What I love about this job is that it gave me the direction and the freedom to pursue the open-ended problems. I think that's where I thrive," he told me while he was explaining his new role.

I'm happy to report that Mike is still in his new role and loving every second of it. He says that he couldn't have done it without the support of his family who was with him during all of his career transitions.

Mike's story is very similar to those in the rest of this book. Early on, he set forth on a path of his own choosing. He was agile, mindful, trusting, and able to make complex choices quickly. From his time at the public school all the way until his current role, he looked into the future and evaluated where he was and where he wanted to go.

One of his most agile periods was when he was getting his graduate degree and working at a different higher educational institution across the street. He was able to pivot to that role so efficiently that it ended up landing him a job at Goldman Sachs.

Also, his story is a tale of networking. People and relationships matter a lot, especially when you are in need of work after a reduction in force or layoff. Through his contacts at Caltech, he was able to truly further his career when he needed the support the most.

Tip for Clocking Out

"What I love about this job is that it gave me the direction and the freedom to pursue the open-ended problems. I think that's where I thrive." Mike's story is all about agility, though he also had to maintain many of the other principles, too. For example, his mindset was always on the horizon, ensuring that he maintained jobs where he could grow. If he wasn't growing, he'd seek something new out. Agility, as you can see, is intimately tied with choice and trust. He makes choices, trusts them, and moves forward. Agility isn't about taking on a bunch of different roles or making choices on a whim. Instead, it's all about a combination of principles that must align if success is going to be achieved. Mike, for instance, always looked for roles where he could thrive and be at his best and he made quick, smart choices (agility) to get where he needed and wanted to go.

10

Matthew Levy:
Adversity and Lily Pads

*"Experience is not what happens to you, it is
what you do with what happens to you."*

—Aldous Huxley

Matthew Levy is a personal friend whom I met many years after my move to the Northeast. Matt and I spent time together on a non-profit board, the Philadelphia Society of People & Strategy (PSPS). During our time as board colleagues, I didn't realize that my then great friend almost left this world very abruptly at a very young age.

Though Matt's career exemplifies most of the principles in this book, he really showcases agility and trust. Over the course of his working life, he's managed to take on a mindset that embraces hardship, which allows him to be extremely agile because he doesn't falter while taking risks.

For some, adversity is frowned upon, but not for Matt. He, unlike so many others, values, learns from, and seeks out adversity because, to him, you cannot have the highs without the lows.

This mindset first started in childhood. Matt grew up as a latchkey kid in Philadelphia. His mother was a homemaker who volunteered with many feminist organizations in the area, and his father was an attorney who passed when Matt was at the tender age of 7.

After this tragic event, Matt's mom took on a part-time role as a secretary to keep the family afloat. Matt says he doesn't remember all that much from this time in his life, but he does know, based on what others have said around him, that it was turbulent.

Matt was the youngest of three children, having two sisters who were 11 and 8 when he was born. He remembers having to come home from school, let himself into the house, make dinner, and generally watch after himself while his mom worked, coming home later in the day.

He believes that this very early experience helped him understand what it took to be independent and get things done.

When he was a bit older, one of Matt's very first jobs was baby-sitting, but his first "real job" came when he was still very young, at the age of 12. The job, which lasted just a single day, was as a busboy at a local restaurant. He remembers that he loaded up his tubs and trays with too many dishes, dropped them on the floor, got embarrassed, and never went back after clocking out that first day.

During this time, he also attended an all-boys school but struggled to feel like he fit into the mold, saying that he felt like an outsider from the wrong part of town. These feelings ebbed when he was "tricked," in his words, by his mom who sent him to an "overnight" camp, which turned out to be much longer. However, once there, he immediately felt like he belonged, taking a leadership role and eventually helping him overcome the things that bothered him at home and at school.

When it came time for college, Matt knew immediately that he wanted to be in business, saying that he always knew the value of providing for himself and his family. What better course of action is there than understanding the business world? From his experience at camp, he also knew that he wasn't the most analytical person. Instead, he loved people, teamwork, and management, which also fed into his business ambitions.

To that end, he obtained a business degree from Ithaca College. Afterward, he returned to Philly where he took up a job in sales after seeing a sign that offered a six- to eight-week sales training course. He figured that he'd give it a shot.

Once actually in the role, Matt flourished, becoming one of the best salespeople on the team. He says that this success stemmed from his ability to hone his skills by listening to others, taking what he thought were good strategies, and applying them himself.

The job, which involved a lot of cold calling, helped him understand how to quickly develop a thick skin. After all, direct selling is a profession that is traditionally looked down upon, with many people thinking salespeople are sleazy liars. Still, with that reputation attached, learning to sell helped Matt understand how to start a dialogue and get ahead even if the cards were stacked against him.

Matt's early life and career all show a key growth mindset, a trait that Matt carries with him wherever he goes. Adversity helps foster growth, spark new ideas, and make every moment one that is worth examining to see what can be gleaned from it.

Alongside his mindset, you can clearly see him being more agile than most here. He took roles where he thought he could grow and become a better professional. He's constantly looking for new ways to improve, especially if they are difficult. Matt's core attitude is basically that nothing in life that is worth doing is easy.

Matt left the sales role after only 18 months, saying that he got all he could out of the role and needed to move on. Following that, he attended a retail executive training program, eventually leading him to the wild world of retail. Again, Matt flourished here, quickly moving up the ranks and into management.

It was at this time that he started having thoughts about the HR world because being a manager at a large retail store involves a lot more HR skills than one might think. He had to hire people, train people, deal with staff issues, and do everything else under the sun.

Back then, the HR function lacked a lot of the formal training options that are around today. So, instead of taking a course, Matt ended up working his way up in the department store until he found himself running the HR functions for 200 people. At this point, his main priority was recruiting, which is now referred to as talent acquisition.

While in this role, he became more and more interested in other HR functions. Talent acquisition, he says, can lead to a lot of burnout. He knew that he had to eventually move into other roles. So, after thinking it over, he eventually asked his boss if he could slowly move into a generalist role where he could perform other duties like employee relations, salary administration, compensation planning, and other skills. He took to these duties like a fish to water.

Matt is a strong believer that passion is a huge differentiator. "Sure," he says, "you do need baseline skills to get your foot in the door, but if you really have passion for what you're doing, it's a lot easier to move into the role you want."

This, he says, is where he learned to sell himself, a skill set that is needed in any business environment. However, HR professionals—unlike others in other roles—typically feel like their work should speak for itself. That, to Matt, is not the case. In order to succeed, you need to be able to market yourself.

After gaining some valuable experience in retail, Matt quickly moved into the pharma world, working for some of the biggest players around. Around this time, Matt got **agile**.

Agility can come in many forms. For Matt, his dive into the pharma world required him to take many risks and adapt extremely quickly. The first agile decision he made was to leave one big pharma company in Pennsylvania and move his family to California to work for a different major pharma company there.

There are a couple things going on here. One is that Matt is trusting himself and the process by taking a new role across the country. At the same time, he is being extra agile, looking for opportunities that some people may have passed on because of the amount of time and energy that one would need to pack up and move such a great distance.

I mentioned to Matt that the move he made from Pennsylvania to California reminded me of my move from the Deep South to the Northeast. On the surface, a move like this seems incredibly exciting, but what lies below the surface is fear and anxiety.

For Matt and his family, they didn't fall in love with their new home. Plus, Matt was hearing rumblings that there were going to be layoffs. All of this culminated in him being recruited from his job in California and relocating back to his home turf in Philly.

While this may seem like a blip on the radar, it's actually a fascinating look at how agile Matt truly is. He saw a new opportunity, went for it, figured out it wasn't working both on a family and business level, and quickly adapted, moving back to Philly and actually finding a new job in the same space. What Matt didn't know at the time was the move to California would end up paving the way for the most incredible opportunity later in his life.

Once back in the familiar ground and in a familiar business, Matt got to work further developing his HR career. At this point, the year was 2008 and as the calendar turned to 2009, Matt had no idea what was around the corner.

As we all now know, around that very corner was the worst economic period in U.S. history since the Great Depression.

Yes, shortly after returning from across the country and landing yet another new role in a big player in the pharma space, Matt— alongside the rest of the country—was about to experience the huge economic tidal wave.

His company was hit with layoff after layoff after layoff. This issue was compounded by the fact that Matt worked in recruiting, an HR function that was all but abandoned once the economic woes started across the nation.

Matt doesn't fully remember the day the call came down that he, too, was let go, but he does remember hearing the normal, standard script that all HR departments seem to use to deliver the news. He walked back to his desk in a daze, gathered his things, and got into his car to go home.

Matt and I reflected together on the emotions one feels when hearing the news you're no longer wanted and your career with the company has now come to an end. We both grew up in HR and have had to deliver the layoff news to hundreds of employees over our combined careers, but it's so very different when you're on the receiving end.

There are certain situations in life where people understand what's happened before anyone even speaks to them. When Matt walked through his front door early that morning, his wife looked at him, knowing what he was about to say already, and asked him, "What happened?"

A sorrowful hug later, Matt, like many who were laid off during the time, turned inward. Why me? Why now? Why is this happening? The next couple of hours were grim.

But Matt isn't a grim person. After coping for a few hours, he quickly came to the realization that this isn't the mindset someone should be in. After working in HR all of those years, he knew that layoffs weren't personal. They weren't targeting him directly and there was nothing he could do, on a personal level, to avoid it. So why sit around moping?

This is a prime example of Matt using his mindset to move forward. He wasn't going to blame others and let this event define who he was as a person. There's no way giving up and quitting was an option. Matt's a hard worker who believes in effort and hard work, and setbacks should be viewed as opportunities for growth. It's easy to sit around and mope, but if you want to change your situation, you need to get up, dust off, and get to work, which is exactly what he did.

His first approach was to simply Google: "How to get a job in the recession?" After some research, he came to the conclusion that there wasn't a silver bullet answer here, though one of the best things he could do was to start to network more heavily.

Then an idea struck him. There were a lot of people in this situation alongside him. Many of these people did not have the HR background that he'd obtained. So why not try to help?

To that end, Matt went about launching his own career coaching firm called Corner Office Career Coaching. Matt figured, "If there's anybody who should be able to get through a layoff, it's me." He had been on both sides of the fence. He'd hired people, laid them off, and generally knew the ins and outs of the entire process. It was now time for him to put all of that knowledge to work. Plus, his company gave him six to eight months of severance, enough to allow him to spread his wings a bit.

Though he was having success helping other people through these tough times, Matt was one of the lucky ones who eventually landed a new role at the very same company that laid him off. He had made an impression and now, with the economy coming back slowly but surely, they wanted him back.

Jumping ahead, Matt worked for the company for a few more years. At this time, in 2013, he was beginning to feel that very same itch he felt way back in his selling days: Is it time that I moved on? Am I really going to work here for the rest of my life?

If there is one thing everyone should know about Matt, it's that he is always in growth mode. If a situation stops pushing him into the future, he looks for ways to better himself elsewhere. This doesn't always mean hopping jobs. Matt's a big proponent of side hustle culture, saying that it's important to be well-rounded and have diverse interests. Plus, it shows that you aren't a one-trick pony.

Still, while working for the pharma company, he asked himself quite often if this was just another lily pad, a term he uses to describe the stepping stone nature of moving up in a corporate environment.

"Just like every other job I have. Whether it worked out or not, it will get me to another lily pad," he said.

He followed up by saying that his mindset is not easily obtained. It takes real courage and **trust** to leave an organization that has a great reputation, a high salary, and amazing benefits, especially when you have children, a house, and other responsibilities.

Still, he always worried about dying with regrets. He didn't want to look back on his life and wonder, "What if?" At this point, he was still very much on the fence. Should he continue his nice, comfortable job? Was it the right time to leave? Would it ever be?

This was on his mind near the end of 2014 when life would hand him his biggest challenge yet and put a razor-sharp edge on his decisions.

One day, while shaving in the bathroom, he noticed a small lump on his neck. Though he felt completely fine, he decided that he should probably have it checked out by his doctor. After numerous tests a few weeks later, his doctor came back to him with horrible news.

Matt was diagnosed with stage IV non-Hodgkin lymphoma, a type of blood cancer that starts in the body's immune system cells. In Matt's case, cancer had spread throughout his entire body. His chances were slim.

Matt was told that he had only 90 days to live.

Even with this intense timeframe, Matt underwent extensive chemotherapy that the doctor said may save his life.

Matt was admitted to the hospital, a place that he wasn't sure he'd ever leave alive. One day, while sitting in his hospital bed watching the outside world go about their business—an activity that Matt did regularly—he started thinking.

Every day, he saw the people of Philadelphia scurrying to and from work. How many of those people down there were going off to do something that they truly cared about? How many of them were stuck on a lily pad, thinking that they had no options? Did any of them really care about what they spent 40 plus hours per week doing?

"How many of those people down there are just going through the motions? Are any of them thinking that they are going to their true calling?" Matt said recently.

Feeling a pit well in his stomach, he thought, "Very few are thinking about their true calling. How many people down there breathe in their calling?"

"If I get the hell out of here, if I get a second chance at life, I must find a way to be one of those very few people who breathe the air of a calling. Not just a job," he told himself.

Eventually, Matt's treatment took. He beat a diagnosis that all but pronounced him dead. And this experience had an obvious impact, teaching him something that many of us think we already know, but likely do not fully understand: life is too short.

Despite the life-changing event that happened to him, Matt makes clear that people do not have to have a near-death experience to change their lives. Everyone, he says, is fighting their own battles. Job loss, for example, can feel like a near-death experience to other people. In any case, it's all about what you do with those moments, whatever they happen to be, not about what the moment is itself.

"If you can picture it, you have the possibility to create it for yourself," Matt said when talking about envisioning a new future for one's self.

Once he got his strength back, he seriously started to consider his next steps. He was no longer a fence-sitter. He was ready to take the leap to the next pad and do something that really meant something to him.

He took another job at a small firm that specialized in HR consulting. Here, he could use his skills to help a bunch of other companies. Even though he felt like he had a bigger impact at this company, he also knew that it still wasn't the end for him.

It was around 2016, and he had left his corporate job for something smaller, but he still didn't know what way he should go. What would really make him feel like he could make a difference with his skills?

Then, one day, the answer that was sitting in front of him the whole time became crystal clear. He should work for a blood cancer–fighting biotech company. What better way to help other people than to help, in his way, to fight the very disease that almost took it all away?

To meet that goal, Matt turned to his network, a faithful strategy that Matt had employed multiple times over the course of his career. After finding four or five companies who were striving to defeat blood cancer, Matt turned to LinkedIn and other networking tools to attempt to get his foot in the door.

A funny thing happened next. While interviewing for a role at one of the companies, Matt realized that the person in charge of hiring was actually an employee of his from 12 years ago at the pharma company in California.

Over a decade later, this person would help Matt join up with the new company. "Be nice to people on your way up the ladder because you may see them on your way down," Matt said.

Matt explained that he would basically do any sort of HR role that the company needed. What was important to him was that he was working for the company because he believed so strongly in their goal and was also a cancer survivor himself.

Admitting that part to a hiring manager can be tough. In fact, a lot of people shy away from explaining their health to employers because it works against them. Matt is not one of these people. His battle with cancer made him who he is. He would never shy away from that.

After interviewing with the company, Matt was hired and onboarded to the team.

Looking back, Matt says that he isn't anyone special. He's a kid from Philly who had his fair share of adversity. What makes Matt different, though, is how he uses adversity as fuel. Matt welcomes adversity at every turn because he knows it is a sure-fire way from lily pad to lily pad, moving up with every hop.

To that end, Matt wants everyone to look at adversity in a different light. Instead of sitting around and wondering why things happen to you, take a step back and realize that adversity is oftentimes a blessing in disguise, presenting a pathway forward that you may have missed if you grew too complacent.

He ends by saying that adversity happens whether we're ready for it or not. It's better to embrace it and change with it than it is to fight it or do nothing. At the end of the day, we all have choices.

"Life, the human existence, is about dealing with adversity. Name someone who goes from birth to death and avoids all adversity. I don't think that person exists," he said.

Matt's story showcases many of the principles. However, his agility really stands out. Even when faced with incredible adversity, Matt is able to read the angles and pick the correct path. In fact, even if it isn't the correct path, Matt still takes the risk and if it doesn't work out, he will learn from it and move on to the next opportunity.

This ability to take a risk, give it a shot, and move on quickly if it fails is a hallmark move for an agile person. You cannot overthink every little thing if you want to move quickly. However, you can always learn from the missteps. And, at the end of the day, doesn't that make them the correct choice anyway?

Tip for Clocking Out

"Life, the human existence, is about dealing with adversity. Name someone who goes from birth to death and avoids all adversity. I don't think that person exists." Matt's ability to focus on adversity—and actually welcome it instead of avoid it—showcases how agile he truly is. When it comes to making agile decisions, many people get caught up in "what if?" scenarios that can make making a choice a lot harder. However, Matt can make choices and deal with the repercussions even if they aren't exactly what he had in mind. Through his mistakes, if you can even call them that, Matt thrives. You can learn a lot by taking risks, but you can also learn a lot about fixing outcomes that you didn't expect. For example, Matt has always been a person to take on new challenges, like moving across the country, but sometimes that didn't work out and he had to adjust. His personal life has also thrown him curveballs, and he was able to keep a positive growth mindset that allowed him to overcome, adapt, and create the future he wanted for himself.

11

Career-minded:
Trust, Giving Up Control

*"Trust the process, one day at a time! What's
for you is for you and no one can stop that."*

—Tony Gaskins

By this point in the Careerminds journey, I've learned that success is a result of hard work and perseverance. The path to achieving success doesn't happen overnight and is not a linear straight line, but a path of unpredictable ups and downs. For some, this can be a difficult climb, because the highs are high and the lows are low. I've also learned that fulfillment isn't necessarily all about achieving goals; it's in knowing that the process, not the outcome, is what's most important, and that process shouldn't be rushed. The hardest part of entrepreneurship is the pressure of feeling that there is so much to do in so little time to find fulfillment. We want so badly to not fail, but to win. Simon Sinek, author of *The Infinite Game*, says, "Finite players play to beat the people around them. Infinite players play to be better than themselves. No matter how successful we are in life, when we die, none of us will be declared the winner of life."

In my mind, fulfillment means trusting the process and taking the time to enjoy what we're learning, appreciating how we're growing from experiences, and that trusting the process is what really matters. Once you finally reach your goal, take time to breathe the fresh air, celebrate and treat yourself to a pat on the back. This was something I didn't do early on, but definitely do more of today with my team.

By the summer of 2009, we had much to celebrate as we landed about a dozen new clients, with our largest account being about $50,000. Despite some quick small-scale success, we recognized that in order for us to really take the company to the next level, we would need to further invest in the product and hire a direct sales and marketing team. We recognized that the concept of "virtual outplacement" delivery was ahead of its time. We also learned that when companies are going through a layoff, they generally use their existing outplacement provider and are not in search of something new. Much of the business we obtained was through companies who had never had layoffs or used outplacement before. We struggled with converting existing users of outplacement. In order for us to flip companies from brick and mortar outplacement to virtual outplacement, we needed to educate the market on the benefits and reasons they should consider it, which would require capital.

At this point, I owned 100 percent of the company and the idea of giving up any part of it for an exchange of venture capital was not something I had given much thought. On the flip side, the idea of taking out a loan and putting up my home as collateral was not something Abby would have supported either. This created quite the situation. In order to grow, I had to choose something. We needed the money if we were to be fully successful.

We did have one big thing going for us: Careerminds was very early to market with the idea of virtual outplacement. Although the recession came upon us quickly, the HR community was very much still used to traditional brick and mortar outplacement with a high touch, face-to-face delivery model.

After weighing the pros and cons for a while, I made the decision to seek outside capital. With Justin having VC experience at TX, he was helpful in putting together a great business plan and pitch deck for potential investors to review. In the early part of 2009, we met some investors through contacts we made at the University of Delaware. The first investor firm we pitched to was Innovation Ventures, which was an early-stage venture fund run by two partners: David Freshman, a well-respected investor in Delaware, Philadelphia, and New York, and Patrick Foley, a retired DuPont executive and investor.

With all of our ducks in a row, on one spring morning in 2009 in the offices of Innovation Ventures, Justin and I pitched David and Pat the Careerminds virtual outplacement model. I was so nervous. I never took one business course in college or even grad school. I studied psychology and the arts—not how to build a pitch deck or a business plan. What did I know about pitching to high-profile investors? Luckily, I had Justin to fall back on. He had the confidence of an old pro. His support and guidance through our first round were paramount to our success.

We arrived with our slides and business plan and started the pitch. I opened by introducing myself as Raymond Lee, founder and CEO of Careerminds, a leading provider of virtual outplacement solutions. I delivered my introduction with confidence as if I had been saying it for many years. Little did they know, I wasn't even sure what virtual outplacement even meant at this point. Needless to say, David and Pat were intrigued by our presentation and especially by how well it played into the currently depressed market. Again, we were introducing a product during the worst recession in modern times. Except, unlike other products, this one was tailor-made to fit inside the economic landscape. There was solid proof that the world needed better, more well-thought-out outplacement right now, not just later, once the economy rebounded.

To give you a sense of just how bad the economy was back then, the market cap for outplacement was a whopping $3 billion because people were using traditional services so often. The three main players at the time, who occupied a third of the market, were Lee Hecht Harrison (LHH), Right Management, and Drake Beam Morin (DBM). DBM would be later acquired by LHH, and that would leave two traditional giants in the outplacement market.

By the end of the meeting, David and Pat said they were interested in continuing conversations, but it wasn't a done deal. They still needed to do some due diligence on Careerminds, us (as people), and the market. They weren't just going to open up their checkbooks and sign a check over to us for a couple million bucks without getting to know us first.

Interestingly, David Freshman shared with us that he worked with a guy years ago who used to run one of the large outplacement firms, Right Management. His name was John "Jack" Gavin. David worked for Jack at Arthur Anderson early in his career, before Jack joined the outplacement juggernaut. David was quite confident that if Jack heard our pitch and agreed with our methods and findings, we would receive a check from Innovation Ventures for $500,000 to get us started.

But that was just the start. The entire plan was to raise over $2 million in Series A from several investors around Philadelphia and New York, with Innovation Ventures in the lead. A few weeks later, David Freshman coordinated a meeting with Jack in Center City Philadelphia to learn about Careerminds. Up to this point, I had thought the investor meeting with David and Pat was the most important meeting in my career. However, it occurred to me a few weeks later that my pitch to Jack Gavin, an outplacement veteran who was instrumental in selling Right Management to Manpower in January of 2004 for over $500 million, was about to determine the fate of both Careerminds and myself.

I spent the first few minutes sharing my experience with outplacement at Corning and in HR at the numerous other places I worked. I also shared how I envisioned the future of today's modern-day job seeker and how career transition and outplacement needed to evolve. I shared that the traditional outplacement model was ripe for disruption. The primary drivers for market disruption were today's modern-day job seekers, who were tech-savvy and capable of using more technology in their job search. Job seekers were networking online using LinkedIn, Facebook, and other social platforms, and lastly, more and more job seekers wanted flexibility in how they connected with their resume writer and career coach. Working virtually was becoming more and more of a demand for employees.

I shared a high-level demo of the product and concept of the delivery model being a social learning management platform that blends high tech job search tools with virtual career consulting and community support. I thought it went well, to say the least.

After the pitch, Jack sat back in his chair, paused looking directly at me, and said: "This is exactly what I was afraid of when I was running Right Management! I was afraid that something better, faster, and disruptive would come into the market. Thankfully, we exited and sold to Manpower before that occurred." What a relief! This was music to my ears.

We continued the discussion and made plans for what we were going to use the venture capital for in terms of growth. Jack agreed that this modern-day approach to outplacement was timely and he conveyed his interest in wanting to get involved. I was not only ecstatic that Jack thought it was a great idea, but that he was also willing to invest his own personal money in the company and put his name and reputation behind our cause.

Once David and Pat returned to the Innovation Ventures office in Delaware, they handed me a term sheet with an investment offer with only days to consider it. The investment offer would be to provide over $2 million in growth capital by May 2011, which would include an investment from Jack and several other investors in the region. It was all happening so fast and was very exciting.

I needed to find a company attorney to help me through the process. I had a handful of Philadelphia attorneys to consider. I talked to everyone who was recommended as I felt like I needed to get as much experience as I could around term sheets and raising venture capital. Going through the process of interviewing attorneys was an experience in and of itself. I could have gone with any of them, as they were all very smart and well-credentialed, but my choice boiled down to one thing: chemistry.

The attorney I hired to help me through the funding process was Jay Coogan, a Tulane University law graduate from New Orleans. Jay also went to Jesuit High School and loved the Saints. Our shared past caused an instant connection. I knew I could trust his judgment from the very start. I did, after all, have a tough decision to make. I was about to sign away over half the company for over $2 million in venture capital. I wasn't just selling off a percentage of my business, I was giving up control of the company. I recognized in order for me to take the company to the next level, I needed to do this and *"trust the process."*

However, I was incredibly nervous about selling off over 50 percent of the company and losing control.

Trust is the fourth principle and was such a critical trait to have at this point in my career because, in order for Careerminds to be successful, I needed to trust my judgment and trust the process, the people around me, my investors, and anyone whom I interacted with on Careerminds.

The other concept I learned and adopted was an internal locus of control. Over time, I've come to believe that the success I achieved in my career and in my company was not a result of luck, but a result of effort and hard work. On the flip side, when I felt insecure about leaving my corporate HR job to go out on my own, I made sure I had a backup plan because I was displaying an external locus of control.

This meant that if I was faced with disappointment and adversity, I wouldn't have the power to change things, therefore needing to revert back to my old job and routine. After I took the risk and learned to trust the process, I discovered that my efforts would lead to success and the luck that appeared along the way was icing on the cake. Whether you're advancing your career or starting a new business, it is important to try to work toward adopting an internal locus of control by practicing self-talk to reinforce your decisions and problem-solving skills. It's also important to set short- and long-term goals for yourself so you can control the direction and successes you're accomplishing.

When working with employees who lose their jobs, we often say to displaced employees, trust the process; you will be much better off in the long run. The problem is that it's hard to trust the process when there is clear uncertainty of the future. That is where the growth mindset and adopting an internal locus of control comes into play. You must not rely on luck and develop a plan of action to move forward with a plan, effort, and hard work.

> *"To have faith is to trust yourself to the water.*
> *When you swim you don't grab hold of the*
> *water, because if you do you will sink and*
> *drown. Instead, you relax, and float."*
>
> —Alan Wilson Watts

Have you ever put up with a hard diet only because you were 100 percent sure that the weight loss or getting in shape would be worth it?

Have you ever endured a long drive, bus, train or a long flight only because you kept reminding yourself of the beautiful destination awaiting you at the end of that long journey?

These are very basic examples, but the point is with hard work and perseverance and "trusting the process," you develop a strong, resilient, and almost unshakable faith that keeps you going through thick and thin with little complaints, only because you've been constantly reminding yourself about the end destination that you were sure you'd arrive at.

In May 2011, just one month after my second child, Matthew, was born, I was signing a contract with the venture capital investors who believed in me and believed in the future of the company. I had to just *"trust the process"* and know that if I worked hard, was open to feedback, and made good choices, I would arrive at a favorable destination.

Tip for Clocking Out

"It is better to own a small percent of something really big versus owning 100 percent of nothing." My vision for Careerminds was to be bigger than life, bigger than me. However, as a naïve entrepreneur, I wanted to be in charge of everything and I wanted to have full control. Giving up that control seemed impossible to do, but I realized that this type of thinking restricted me from actually growing to the next level. Finding and partnering with the right investors and board would prove to be the right decision to position the company for growth and success.

Todd Bieber: Trust Every Step

"The world breaks everyone and afterward many are strong at the broken places."

—Ernest Hemingway

Trust may be the hardest principle to follow in this book. It can be incredibly challenging when faced with a difficult situation to allow the process to unfold. Trust is also an incredibly personal thing.

When you start a career, you are already starting to trust the process. You are trusting that if you work hard, learn from your mistakes, and take special care to plan and look ahead, things will always work out.

What does that mean? Well, trust—like agility—is a mindset in and of itself. If you never trust the process, you will likely never switch into growth mode because any time there is a choice to be made, you will clam up and not be able to push forward. Trust is all about taking educated risks to be agile or to trust the process set in front of you, whether that be your own personal plan or a plan set forth by a career coach.

I met Todd Bieber though a longtime career coach and friend. I was personally moved by Todd's story and career transition.

Todd Bieber grew up just west of Sylvania, Ohio, in a house on 11 acres of land that had woods and a stream in the back, the perfect place to run about as a child.

He was the middle child with an older brother and younger sister. His parents have been married for over 40 years. His father was an electrician and his mother, a teacher. Todd says that his father was an incredibly hard worker who took on side gigs after work to provide for the family, create opportunities for involvement in travel sports, and improve the house.

Todd says that this work ethic has been instilled into him. No matter what Todd does, he goes in full tilt. All of his heart and energy go into his tasks, and this, to him, was all from his father, much to the chagrin of his wife.

Todd's thankful that he has such a tight-knit family. He's worked with his older brother's landscaping business multiple times throughout his life and is very appreciative to have him as a supporter. His sister, who is a fitness instructor, homeschools her children and is a key part in keeping the entire family in close contact. He has no complaints about his family, saying that he is lucky to have them. In fact, all of his family members still live within a short drive of each other, and Todd lives in his father's old house, which they are working on remodeling.

Growing up, Todd says he had the "distorted" idea to be a pro athlete. But like many childhood dreams, he realized that that wasn't really possible despite the fact that a college teammate of his was drafted into the MLB. Still, he did have a decent baseball career at Tri-State University (a Division II school in Indiana) and after transferring to the University of Toledo as a walk-on, practiced with the team for two years and was then offered a student assistant coaching role.

That role, though, didn't pay and took up a lot of time. This helped Todd realize that he needed another option, so he majored first in engineering and then in mathematics education. He was good at it, but he wasn't excited by it.

So, another major change. This time to physical and health education. Todd realized that he still had a passion for athletics even though he wasn't going to be a pro athlete. With this degree, he could help athletes, teach kids, get paid while doing it, and keep his life moving forward.

Already, you can see Todd being agile. Throughout high school and college, Todd had multiple paths to choose from, but making choices can be hard, to say the least. He weighed his options, made moves, and eventually landed on a role that he really fit into, one that paid well, allowed him to explore his passions, and even kept him in close contact with his family.

During college, he applied his love for athletics to become a personal trainer. Then, after graduating in 2001, he worked in the Toledo Public School system while still doing personal training on the side and working with his brother when he could.

So, why sports? I asked Todd this very question and he had a really good answer. To Todd, sports are a huge deal. He loves the competitiveness, the stories behind the scenes, seeing people work hard together, and how sports can prepare you for a myriad of life events. For him, sports are not something that you watch only on Sunday and then call it a day. If you dig deeper, you can find out a lot about yourself through their application.

During his time at the public school, Todd helped a friend coach baseball for a different school. At his own school, he coached Special Olympics track and basketball. He says that he loved working with disabled athletes. The joy, the passion for the game, and the overall excitement from the community was astounding. He loved that kids came out and played for the love of playing instead of the hyper-competitiveness that pervades most other sports.

After four years working in the Toledo Public School system, Todd applied to move up in the school. He had aspirations of becoming a superintendent one day. However, the school board said that he needed at least five years of teaching, which Todd was one year shy of. They passed on him, though they did give him an interview.

In 2005, Todd left the school system after the school board laid him off. Then, after Todd dropped resumes all over the place, his supervisor called and said that he had another teaching role for him, but that he would likely be in the same situation next year. In other words, he couldn't guarantee that Todd would have a longer-term job.

At this point, Todd had already landed another role outside of teaching as a loan officer for a mortgage company. Todd said that this was a great learning experience, teaching him how to cold call and build relationships quickly. He liked helping people get better loans and buy their houses.

The role allowed him to get outside of his comfort zone and grow as a person. This is another great example of having a growth mindset. Todd was a teacher and a coach, not a salesperson or a banker. This role was outside of the norm for him and many people may have sat around and bemoaned the new position. Not Todd. He looked at this new job as a way to grow a new skill that he could take with him anywhere he went afterward. Todd worked in this role until the end of 2006. His first child was born in early 2005.

Being a loan officer at this time was highly lucrative. Todd says that most of the loan officers he worked with were in their mid-twenties, making over $100K per year, driving fancy cars, and generally living the high life. Todd, on the other hand, wasn't able to do what the other officers did.

He said that he was always honest with people about their loans. He never promised something that wasn't true, and if he couldn't get them to save money, he'd tell them so. As you probably know based on the other stories in this book, mortgage lenders in 2005 and 2006 were setting the stage for a financial collapse towards the end of the decade. Todd, unlike many others I talked with for this book, was on the front lines of this process, though he's careful to note that he really did try to make people's lives better through his work and not take advantage of them even though it felt like everyone else was.

In fact, Todd was impacted by the housing bubble himself. After having his child, he and his wife decided that they needed more space, so they built a new house. At this point, they were paying for two houses during a time when the market was good. However, as you know, everything would come crashing down. Todd says that they lost quite a bit because of it.

To make matters worse, this was right after Todd left the mortgage lending business. Needless to say, it was a hard time. Luckily, he was able to help his brother with his landscaping business mowing lawns.

Todd remembers thinking about all of this one day while mowing the lawn of the church he got married in when he got a phone call. A while ago, he interviewed with a major glass manufacturer and they finally, after what seemed like an eternity, offered him a job.

This is a good moment to talk about trust. Todd left the mortgage lending business for personal reasons. He didn't like the idea of basically scamming people into loans that didn't work for them. He did this despite the fact that he had just had his first child and the economy wasn't looking that good. Still, he managed to patch over his transition period by working for his brother, whom he can't say enough about. He's very grateful. He then waited and trusted that he would get out of this. And he did.

The new role was as a supervisor in the production department. He was excited and scared. He had never worked in manufacturing before, but he was ready to learn. The role required him to take on shifts of 12-plus hours a pop, having three days on and three days off. He said this allowed him to have a lot of free time when he wasn't working. When he was working, he said that there was always a lot to do. Still, Todd is not one to sit around on his days off. Remember his father's work ethic? This is where it comes out.

So, with time off at hand, Todd filled it with more work, starting with a role selling insurance that he found from a friend who was also in the role and making decent money with it. But then his shift schedule changed and he couldn't hold that role anymore. He eventually got a raise and a promotion after his first year at the glass company, allowing him to have a more traditional day job where he could spend more time with his family after work.

Todd says that his time at the glass company was terrific. He moved up and learned at every step. It seems to me that this is a reflection of his coaching past. He loves working with people, learning their roles, and helping the company, too. He always wants to lead by example and help people where he can. With his promotion, he was able to help people even more by bringing people together from all sides of the organization. And it wasn't a small organization, either. At this plant alone, 700 workers performed various roles.

Eventually, he even got to move up to be on global conference calls with plants all over the world. He was now in a leadership role that expanded the globe. It was invigorating. And, just to be clear, when I say that he got promoted, he got promoted four times in the 10 years he was employed there. He started in the production area as a supervisor and was eventually managing a $23 million dollar budget with 20-plus salaried team members and 150-plus hourly team members, working many different roles in the process.

Despite his success, there was always something going on in the company with constant restructuring taking place at every turn.

This meant that Todd was bounced around through roles, which he learned from at every step. He even achieved his master's degree while working at the company. However, one final reorganization changed it all.

With a new CEO and plant manager shaking things up, the company decided that they wanted an outside employee to take over Todd's responsibilities. Todd, who loved the company, attempted to find work elsewhere at the plant, but HR wasn't having it. The company was changing all around him, and Todd was stuck in the center of it all.

So, after 10 years of working at the company, Todd was let go.

When reflecting about this time of his life, Todd goes back to sports. He said that what he loved the most, and what he was able to do at the company, was bring people together just like he had when he was a coach. It was all about teamwork at every level. And despite the fact that he was let go, he has nothing bad to say about the company. He loved it there. He loved the people. He's very proud that many of his employees have stayed there and thrived, moving up into bigger and better roles even though he had to exit.

Though he didn't know what his next step was, he didn't sit around feeling sorry for himself. Instead, he started looking for ways to be an asset somewhere else. And where does Todd go to do some heavy thinking? You guessed it, the lawnmower.

Having his brother there to help during trying times is something that is a constant in Todd's life—one that he is greatly thankful for. This time, he had no idea where his next path would go, but he trusted his own process and knew that something would take him on a new journey, which is exactly what he pondered as he helped mow lawns again.

Before we get into what his next step was, we need to rewind in time for a second to something that we haven't yet discussed. When Todd was still working for the glass company, he found himself in a situation that plagues many but is rarely discussed openly: the throes of addiction.

A combination of alcohol, marijuana, and prescription drugs—prescribed after surgeries Todd had from sports injuries, working out, and working hard labor most of his life. Todd was using multiple substances during the day and night. He told me that he was grateful that his family was always there to attempt to keep him in check, which would cause him to clean up for a few days, but he would also go right back to his old ways.

Todd's addictions to drugs and alcohol eventually led to a car crash in 2013, which served as a big wake up call. At that time, he thought his life was over, that he was a failure, that he didn't have a future.

Now, all of this was during his flourishing time at the glass company. I think it's important to note that here because you never truly know the wars other people are fighting. In Todd's words, this success actually made his problem seem like less of a problem because he was moving up at the company, was getting promotions, had a family—everything was going fine. How could he have a problem? All of this prolonged his attempts at recovery.

The accident put everything into perspective. He got a DUI and lost his license, which meant that he needed rides to work and other things. Todd thought he was completely alone in the world. That he was the only one with a problem.

To help fight his DUI case, he decided to go to addiction meetings, but at this point, he was still lying through his teeth about how much he was drinking and doing drugs. He really only started recovery, he says, as a means to get back to normal with work.

Even though he started the program with the wrong reasoning, once he was getting the treatment it really clicked with him. In fact, I'm very happy to report that Todd has been sober for the last seven years. He even managed to have a major back surgery during this time, was prescribed 160 painkillers, and didn't take any of them.

It's important to note here that this situation is very common in today's world. If you are reading this and you are struggling with addiction, I implore you to go seek help. You are not alone and it is never too late to make the choice.

Todd found the help he needed through an organization called Racing for Recovery, which held meetings and events all over the area. He immediately took to the whole organization, but he was still working at the glass plant. He loved the organization so much that he even volunteered to be on the board of directors, helping them raise funds and help more and more people that were in the same situation that he was in.

However, once he was let go from the glass manufacturer, which gave him six months of severance, he started working with his brother again as I mentioned before. During this time, he was putting out interviews and trying to get a new job. In the back of his mind, though, he wondered if he really wanted to go back to a normal job.

To help himself understand his next step, Todd did some hard thinking, looking over what he loved and what he really wanted to do. He had always loved teaching and coaching. He also performed well and thrived in the manufacturing and business roles that he took on. What to do?

As these thoughts were racing through his head, the man who ran Racing for Recovery, Todd Crandell, was asking him if he'd want to do more for the organization. This was an interesting idea for Todd. He absolutely wanted to help Racing for Recovery as much as he could, but there weren't *real* jobs there that could pay him for his work and things like that.

Eventually, though, after the organization helped a family's loved one with recovery, Racing for Recovery was granted six months' rent at a brick and mortar location where they could actually hold meetings and make an office. In short, they'd have their very own treatment center.

Todd talked over the move into full-time treatment work with his wife Amy and the rest of his family. They backed his decision and Todd went to work with Racing for Recovery at their brand-new location. At this point, there were only three people working there and they were still very much trying to figure out how to make all of this work.

Todd remembers writing the very first paychecks while working there. It was an awesome day. He also remembers donating his first one back to the organization to help support them, an act he was able to do thanks to his severance payments.

Nowadays, Racing for Recovery has over 15 employees and holds meetings for over 30 groups per week. They have two gyms. They do yoga every week. They have parent groups, nutrition groups, educational wellness groups, art therapy, journaling groups, children groups, sports groups, everything.

Todd loves that he can now truly help people with their battle with drugs and alcohol. If you think about it, Todd is doing what it seems like he was destined to do: coach. Sure, this isn't athletics (though they do have a lot of athletic activities), but he is able to use his coaching skills, management skills, and people skills to truly make a difference in the community he loves. Todd, in a nutshell, is all about helping people. Todd credits his parents, siblings, wife, and kids for always being there to support him and keep him working hard in an effort to make them all proud.

You know one thing that Todd still does? Reflect on his lawn-mower. With his family close by, he loves helping whenever he can. He still helps his brother deal with the Ohio snow when he can.

Todd has high hopes for the years to come at Racing for Recovery. He hopes they will be able to help more and more people as they continue to grow with the mindset of simply helping people to become the amazing individuals that they were meant to be.

Tip for Clocking Out

Trust is one of the hardest principles outlined in this book. To trust the process, you must be willing to give up some sort of control. We cannot, after all, control every single aspect of our lives, and we cannot control every part of our careers. However, with a proper mindset and the ability to make quick adjustments (agility), you can start to trust the process and more importantly yourself. Trust comes in many forms. For Todd, he had to trust the process of not only switching jobs but his treatment as well. Specifically for careers, trust comes into play when you make agile choices (trusting yourself), when you create a plan (trusting the process), and when you have a goal far into the future (trusting your mindset).

Mary Evon: Banking on Trust

"Trust the timing of your life. Keep focusing on putting one foot in front of the other, be kind, and follow your heart. Doors will open effortlessly, but first, you have to be ready to walk through."

—Brittany Burgunder

Losing your job is a traumatic thing; you become untrusting of other jobs and people. This was one of the first things Mary Evon told me when we chatted about her career. Her story has many twists and turns, but throughout it all, she's maintained an agile growth mind-set that's propelled her forward.

Still, trust can be a very hard thing to have. If you've been let go before, you know all about this. You can have trouble trusting the process and an even harder time breaking into a growth mind-set after the event. For Mary, this, in her words, is the story of her working life. She had to be agile at every turn to ensure that she kept going forward. Her story shows that if you keep at it, trust yourself, and look for agile moves along the way, you'll always come out the other side.

Let's jump back to the very beginning. Mary grew up in Waterbury, Connecticut, where she still lives to this day. She had an older brother and a younger sister, making her the middle child of three. In Mary's words, her mother described her as an extremely talkative person with a great smile. Mary recalls always being in the hallway after being kicked out of class for talking, but then she would wind up just talking to the janitors out there.

Mary's father was a self-taught plumber who only made it to the eighth grade. Still, despite his lack of formal education, he was a hard worker and go-getter who wouldn't let anything stop him from succeeding. This trait was definitely passed down to Mary. After working alongside another plumber and being taught on the job, her father moved the family into a house that was owned by the company he worked for.

Mary's mother worked part-time for a vending company but was home when her children got out of school during the day. She would volunteer at cupcake and hot dog sales. Her brother—who sadly passed away five years ago due to a heart condition at 55 years old—was also a plumber and made some extra money delivering newspapers with their mom around town.

Mary said that her school life was always a challenge. At age 13, she developed alopecia, a condition that causes hair loss. Back then, though, very few people understood this medical condition and they couldn't find a way to cure Mary's hair loss. She said that she was picked on quite a bit for having to wear a wig, even recalling one time when she was chased in the school hallways. Her brother, she says, protected her as best he could and was even suspended from school over this incident.

Public school wasn't working out, so Mary eventually enrolled in a Catholic school. She's still a practicing Catholic to this day. Still, even with the change, Mary didn't enjoy school at all. Her grades were never that great, averaging out to her being a B or C student. She couldn't wait to leave.

Once she graduated, she stepped right into the banking world. Back then, everything was done via the phone or paper. People would call in or leave messages for transfers and Mary had to write slips out manually for the proof department. She loved this job. She still claims it was one of the best in her career.

Mary continued to progress through the banking world. First, she moved from manually writing slips into the electronic funds department and the lockbox department. In this role, Mary helped deposit company checks after rechecking the addition as they came into the bank.

Everything was going pretty well at this point. At the age of 21, Mary married after communicating with a guy she met on a CB radio channel.

Then, life threw a curveball. In 1987, at the age of 26, Mary was pregnant with her first son when the bank was relocating out of Connecticut. Mary says that this is the story of her life. Every time she gets comfortable something happens with the company she works for and the rug is pulled from underneath her. Often times this was due to the company relocating, which is something that she really doesn't want to do because she loves her life and community in Connecticut. After having her first son, she returned to the bank part-time then went to work at a bunch of smaller stores in the area as she looked for more work. Mary then had a second son in 1990 before beginning a different job in banking.

She eventually landed a job as a teller to another bank for being talkative, just like in school. Mary was never one to shy away from her personal outspoken opinions. She remembers that one time the bank was bought by another bank (a common trend, like she said) and there were a ton of people coming in and out trying to make the switch over to the new company.

During this time, she made it clear that people who worked the front lines of banking needed to be paid more than the people in the back end, a bold claim made even bolder by the fact that Mary worked in the back end of the bank more than the front, though she did help out up there quite often. She saw both sides of the fence and appreciated the experience she gained. The girls at the bank loved her for this and her outspoken nature.

Working at a bank was a really good fit for Mary because she got to see people in the community, help them with their finances, and generally keep an eye out for people around her. One funny story she remembers is of a small, elderly Russian woman who would come into the bank when her Social Security check came and she would take the cash home. This was when paper checks for Social Security were mailed. Mary constantly worried that this lady who would take her whole check out in cash could have gotten robbed. She told her she could come back the next day as she would be there waiting for her. It was these small, yet very personal connections, that seemed to fuel Mary at the bank.

Still, Mary eventually left the role in 2008 and became an imaging specialist at a chemical company after starting off as a temp-to-perm person. For those who aren't familiar, imaging specialists would take invoices that came in the mail, then scan them into the company's systems for further processing by an accounts payable clerk. Mary remembers the absolute ton of mail she used to receive on Monday mornings. Back then, she recalls, email was still shunned and most people still sent physical letters for invoices, or they'd send an email and an invoice just to make sure, which wasn't an easy issue to deal with to prevent duplicate entries.

Mary worked this role for a while then applied to move into accounts payable. This was a logical step because she already knew everything about the department from being an imaging specialist. It was a no-brainer for her to level up her career and take on this new role.

This is just an early example of Mary's mindset. She saw an opportunity and she took it, knowing that she would learn on the go just like her father did with plumbing. Being agile and trusting that you have what it takes to pull something off is a skill, and Mary is showcasing that here.

But life wasn't done yet. Mary ended up working in this role for just about 10 years, all the way up until 2018 when the CEO announced that the company would be sold off to another chemical company that was based in Germany. This meant that Mary was soon to be out of a job again after nearly a decade of consistent work.

To make matters more frustrating, the German company did have a presence already in Pittsburgh, Pennsylvania. Mary's department would basically move there, something that Mary didn't want to do at all because of family.

She was given six months' notice and was told that if she stayed to see the transition through that she would be given a severance package.

Here is where we really see what Mary is made of. During this transition period, Mary and the other people in her department were tasked with training the Pittsburgh employees who were taking their jobs. These workers would come out to Connecticut and work alongside Mary and her crew, trying to get all of the details ironed out about the role.

Most people would hate this. Why should they have to train the very people who were taking their jobs away? Was this some kind of joke? But Mary didn't feel this way. Like every role, she gave it her all. Still, there were issues. While the girl she was training was nice and friendly, the manager from Pittsburgh was very rude to Mary and her fellow workers. So much so that Mary eventually had to go to her manager and tell them what was going on. They eventually solved the situation, but Mary, being Mary, was still looking out for her coworkers.

After training, the girl from Pittsburgh worked alongside Mary for two months, ensuring that she had everything figured out. Mary recalls that the girl was quite surprised that Mary was able to get everything done every day—it just seemed like far too much work for one person.

Mary told her that she just needed to stick with it and she'd get better, remembering all of the times she made a small mistake and would be kicking herself over it at home that night. But because of her great mindset, Mary took all of her mistakes as opportunities to grow and develop her skills.

Though she became good friends with her replacement, Mary decided to keep the relationship strictly professional and not over-step bounds by allowing the girl to have her personal phone number. She knew that the girl would be great but didn't want to keep working for the organization after she left by answering countless phone calls about her old role. It was nothing personal—Mary just had to move on.

In April 2018, Mary made her full exit from the company. She managed to stay on board to the very end to ensure that she received her severance package.

After searching during her final months at the chemical company, Mary eventually landed a new role as an accounts payable clerk at a construction company. Mary laughs and says that this very same company actually turned her down when she first applied while still at the chemical company.

Mary was pretty happy in this role and thankful to have a steady job while also getting severance. She was able to continue learning new skills at this job and thought everything was going well until 2019 when, yet again, the company announced that her position was being eliminated at the corporate office.

The exit from the construction company wasn't nearly as chaotic as the one from the chemical company. Instead, it was pretty standard. They offered her severance and outplacement from Careerminds. Still, after nearly a year, Mary was once again unemployed, a situation that is stressful no matter what.

Mary says that it was a big struggle at first. She remembered the time when you could get up in the morning, dress up, and hit the pavement, dropping off resumes at local businesses in person. This had changed completely.

Nowadays, LinkedIn, job boards, social media, and networking are how many people find work, and this was completely outside of Mary's wheelhouse.

To make matters worse, the job she was used to having in accounts payable was slowly but surely disappearing. Those roles are now done in the field where each project or job is happening. Mary's role, in other words, was starting to disappear as a profession. This was made all the harder by the fact that Mary had to begin a new job search again.

So, Mary did what anyone would do. She made a LinkedIn account with the help of Careerminds and started looking for work online. She contacted recruiting agencies and went to countless interviews. Still, even with all of this hard work, nothing was coming. Two months into her job hunt, she decided to pivot. With the internet not working out for her, she needed a new strategy.

She decided to call up temp agencies on Tuesdays. Why? Because Mondays were notoriously busy for them, so she wanted to get them while they were cooling off. After some trial and error, she discovered that Tuesday was the best day.

Around this time, Mary says that she saw herself change. She stopped looking at the job hunt in the same way and started to get more aggressive with agencies to help her find a job. She also stopped relying solely on applying to jobs online and waiting for a callback. The black hole of job applications was very real and discouraging. One day Mary mapped out all of the businesses in her area and got in the car and drove from business to business dropping off a resume in person and expressing her desire for work. This door-to-door approach was Sales 101 and demonstrates her commitment to finding a job. This is also a clear example of agility and mindset working together. She saw that one strategy wasn't working and needed to change it quickly.

Though everything was still a challenge, her new mindset helped her be as agile as possible, always looking for ways to game the system to her favor. She claims that being a "big mouth," as people call her, helped out a lot here. Basically, Mary let go of the break and became her authentic self while looking for a new role. She wasn't going to take no for an answer.

At the same time, she was working with a career coach from Careerminds who was helping her create a strategy. This is where trust comes into play, too. She trusted the job search system and even changed it to meet her needs, but she knew that if she kept working at it she would land a role sooner or later. She hoped it would be sooner.

A while later, she eventually landed a new role through the temp agency by looking for roles that she could fulfill with her experience in accounts payable. Accounts payable, as I said before, is a profession that has switched to part-time over the last couple of years. So, Mary had to use her transferrable skills to land a new job that had a more clear-cut future.

Mary says that she really doesn't want to work for corporations anymore after all of the pivots and job loss events that she's had to deal with, but she's happy knowing that she can develop new skills to help future-proof herself against those pivots moving forward.

When asked if she had any tips about how to find a job after years of steady employment, Mary said, like many others I interviewed for this book, that the best thing to do is to start looking for work right away. There's no time to spare and every second counts. You never know how long you will be without work, and you cannot depend on unemployment or agencies to get you there.

Mary is a fan of saying that working and finding a new role is all about putting one foot in front of the other. There is no special strategy that works for everyone, but if you keep going every day, you will get where you need to go.

Mary's story is one that a lot of people can relate to. She didn't go to college, but she spent her career working for good companies and always looked for opportunities to grow and develop her skills. When she found herself down, she found a way to pick herself back up and try different things. She had to choose which direction to go, to be agile when forced into a corner or to understand what paths she could take. She also had to trust herself and the process. If she didn't, she definitely wouldn't be where she is today. All of this was dictated by her incredible growth mindset. She constantly went from one role to the other, perfecting her job. She even did this during her job transition by looking at the process and molding it to fit her needs, which is one of the most agile things a person can do.

I've shared my journey and the story of several brave individuals who had the will to demonstrate how choice, mindset, agility, and trust can be used throughout life.

Ask yourself: Are you currently in a job or career that is not bringing you fulfillment? Have you recently been faced with a job loss or adversity that is challenging to overcome?

So, what do you do now?

What if you made a choice and took a risk to change? What would you do if you clocked out of your company or if you were asked to leave unexpectedly? My hope is that the stories we shared in this book will offer some hope and inspiration that anyone has the power to do extraordinary things. It starts with a choice. Are you willing to make that choice today?

Tip for Clocking Out

Mary exemplifies a high level of trust both with herself and the process. For example, when she was laid off the last time, she had to trust the outplacement process. However, once she was in the program, she started making her own processes and had to trust those, which ultimately worked. Mary's ability to trust helped her gain all the other principles, specifically mindset and agility, which go hand-in-hand when making choices.

Epilogue

I shared the story of my mom, who worked hard to change her career from schoolteacher to court reporting to archeologist. As I mentioned in her story, she graduated with a master's degree in the spring of 2012. I was so proud to watch her walk across the stage to receive her diploma from the University of Southern Mississippi at the age of 60. I wish I could say that my mom had the opportunity to live out her dream of being an archaeologist and working in the field for the years to come, but unfortunately, it didn't end that way. She left the world just six months later due to a sudden terminal illness that surprised us all. In November 2012, she was laid to rest. Just a few months before she left the world, I had the opportunity to spend some quality time with my mom to learn and really appreciate the sacrifices she made for me, my brother, and the rest of the lives she touched. She was a remarkable lady. She left the ones in her life stronger and better people than before.

Over the years, she had always kept the hundreds of love letters that she wrote to her first husband and my dad, Kirk, in a large shoebox. These letters were written over 40 years ago in the early '70s when he was in the Air Force and I was a baby. She presented me with these letters days before her passing, and later my brother, David, and I passed on the letters to my dad in hopes that he'd get the kind of inspiration we received growing up. My dad is now retired and lives in New Orleans. His mother passed several years ago, and he has developed a strong relationship with his stepdad. He has truly transformed as a person and is volunteering his time with church ministry at hospitals and individual nutrition coaching in New Orleans. He's committed to church service, and he is giving back to society. I'm truly proud of who he has become today.

My mom has also been an incredible inspiration to her second husband (and my stepdad) John Hester. I'm grateful for his love of her. They were married for 20 years. He adored her and calls her his wife even today.

Today, my mom would be proud of what I've accomplished. Careerminds has now been in business for over a decade. I'm happy to say that with the support of our employees, clients, career coaches, investors, and the HR community, we've grown to be a leader in our industry, providing virtual outplacement solutions to companies around the world. The term "virtual" would not only become a standard of how outplacement would be delivered, but it would become a new normal for Americans and how we work, play, and interact with one another as defined by a pandemic that would be named COVID-19, also referred to as the coronavirus.

May I ask you a favor? If you enjoyed this book and took something from it, please give it to someone else to read. Life is too short. My hope is that we all can all live out our purpose in life and bring meaning to the world, but it starts with a choice. I ask you to give this to someone so they too can make a choice: a choice for change, a choice to be fulfilled, a choice to have a new career, or a choice to be happy.

About The Author

Raymond Lee is the founder and CEO of Careerminds, a global virtual outplacement company launched in 2008. He has over 18 years of human resource, outplacement, and career consulting experience, and he's also a certified retirement coach.

Raymond pioneered the concept of virtual outplacement after years of delivering traditional outplacement in a variety of HR roles, and saw a huge opportunity to align career transition programs with the way people were actually looking for jobs. When Raymond started the company, he had one goal in mind: to create forward-thinking transition programs that reduced employee stress. This included developing robust software to personalize the transition experience for all levels of the organization and hiring expert consultants to support participants every step of the way.

Raymond holds his bachelor's in psychology and a master's degree in industrial/organizational psychology from Louisiana Tech University. He sits on the Careerminds Board of Directors, is the past president of the Philadelphia Society of People and Strategy, and is an active speaker and contributor to HRPS & SHRM. Raymond's been featured on SiriusXM Business Radio, the Wall Street Journal, CNN Business, and Fox Business News.

Raymond lives outside Philadelphia with his wife, Abby, daughter, Rachel, and son, Matthew.

Index